Day One: **Data Center Fundamentals**

By Colin Wrightson

Chapter 1: Common Components 9
Chapter 2 : Architectures 19
Chapter 3: Cabling 27
Chapter 4: Oversubscription 33
Chapter 5: Fabric Architecture 45
Chapter 6: IP Fabrics and BGP 65
Chapter 7: Overlay Networking 79
Chapter 8: Controllers 93
Chapter 9: EVPN Protocol 107
Summary 121

© 2016 by Juniper Networks, Inc. All rights reserved.
Juniper Networks and Junos are registered trademarks of Juniper Networks, Inc. in the United States and other countries. The Juniper Networks Logo, the Junos logo, and JunosE are trademarks of Juniper Networks, Inc. All other trademarks, service marks, registered trademarks, or registered service marks are the property of their respective owners. Juniper Networks assumes no responsibility for any inaccuracies in this document. Juniper Networks reserves the right to change, modify, transfer, or otherwise revise this publication without notice.

Published by Juniper Networks Books
Author & Illustrations: Colin Wrightson
Technical Reviewers: Anoop Kumar Sahu, Oliver Jahreis, Guy Davies, Thorbjoern Zieger, Bhupen Mistry
Editor in Chief: Patrick Ames
Copyeditor and Proofer: Nancy Koerbel

ISBN: 978-1-941441-39-8 (paperback)
Printed in the USA by Vervante Corporation.

ISBN: 978-1-941441-40-4 (ebook)
Version History: v1, September 2016

About the Author
Colin Wrightson is a Consultant System Engineer with the EMEA Center of Excellence team focusing on data center product and design and has been with Juniper Networks for over six years. His previous roles within Juniper have been Systems Engineer and Senior Systems engineer for enterprise covering government and defense sectors. Prior to Juniper he worked for Cisco partners as field engineering, engineering lead, and then pre-sales, before seeing the error of his ways and joining Juniper.

Author's Acknowledgments
I'd like to thank Patrick Ames who has spent far too long correcting my questionable grammar and spelling with the help of Nancy Koerbel. Thank you to the technical reviewers. I'd also like to thank Bhupen (social media assassin) for his continued encouragement during this process, Mark Petrou (big cod), who first gave me the idea for a book, and Starbucks, whose coffee made a lot of early morning writing easier. Last, but most importantly not least, I want to thank my long-suffering and loving wife who makes all of this possible. Oh, and hello to Jason Issacs.

http://www.juniper.net/dayone

Welcome to Day One

This book is part of a growing library of *Day One* books, produced and published by Juniper Networks Books.

Day One books were conceived to help you get just the information that you need on day one. The series covers Junos OS and Juniper Networks networking essentials with straightforward explanations, step-by-step instructions, and practical examples that are easy to follow.

The *Day One* library also includes a slightly larger and longer suite of *This Week* books, whose concepts and test bed examples are more similar to a weeklong seminar.

You can obtain either series, in multiple formats:

- Download a free PDF edition at http://www.juniper.net/dayone.
- Get the ebook edition for iPhones and iPads from the iTunes Store. Search for Juniper Networks Books.
- Get the ebook edition for any device that runs the Kindle app (Android, Kindle, iPad, PC, or Mac) by opening your device's Kindle app and going to the Kindle Store. Search for Juniper Networks Books.
- Purchase the paper edition at either Vervante Corporation (www.vervante.com) or Amazon (amazon.com) for between $12-$28, depending on page length.
- Note that Nook, iPad, and various Android apps can also view PDF files.
- If your device or ebook app uses .epub files, but isn't an Apple product, open iTunes and download the .epub file from the iTunes Store. You can now drag and drop the file out of iTunes onto your desktop and sync with your .epub device.

Audience and Scope of This Book

This book is intended for both Enterprise and service provider engineers, network administrators, network designers/architects, and anyone who wants to understand the basic principles of data center design. This book provides field-tested solutions for common data center network deployment scenarios, as well as the brief background information needed to understand and design these solutions for your own environment.

The chapters of this book are organized in a logical sequence to help provide the reader with a step-by-step understanding of data center design principles and how these principles can then be developed into a solution that fits the role of a modern data center.

What You Need to Know Before Reading This Book

Before reading this book, you should have a basic understanding of network protocols and general design terms. While this book does not cover Junos operating systems and configurations, there are several excellent books on learning Junos in the *Day One* library at at http://www.juniper.net/dayone.

This book makes a few assumptions about you, the reader:

- You have a basic understanding of Internet Protocol (IP) versions 4 and 6
- You have a basic understanding of network design at a campus level
- You work with servers and want to understand the network side of data centers

What You Will Learn by Reading This Book

- Basic principles of data center design and how they have evolved
- How different data center designs affect applications
- What overlay and underlay are, and why they are important
- How Controller and Controllerless networks can improve Layer 2 scale and operations
- A better understanding of Juniper data center products

Preface

This *Day One* book provides you with a thorough understanding of all the components that make up a Juniper Networks data center solution; in essence, it offers a 10,000 foot view of how everything regarding Juniper's data center solution fits together. Such a view enables you to see the value Juniper provides over other vendors in the same space by glimpsing the big picture.

This books starts by covering the basics and slowly builds upon core ideas in order to cover more complex elements. Design examples relate back to an example architecture that is common throughout the book, thus providing an easy reference point to gauge guideline solutions.

The idea is to allow you to design your own network and, in the process, come to understand why you would favor one technology or design principle over another. In order to do that, this book points out subtle differences along the way:

- Chapter One: Common Components starts with the various common components (products) you can use and where they sit in the design topology. This is important because of the differences between merchant silicon and custom silicon, and because different vendors have different approaches and those approaches can affect the network and services you may want to implement.

- Chapter Two: The Top-of-Rack or End/Middle-of-Row chapter looks at the different architectures you can use, depending on your server selection, contention ratio, and overall rack and cabling design.

- Chapter Three: Cabling is sometimes a neglected element of the larger design, but it can have interesting repercussions if not considered.

- Chapter Four: Over Subscription is the first design point to think about when designing a network. If you know the speeds at which your servers are connecting, and the bandwidth they are going to need, not just on day one but also ex-number of years from now, then you can start the design process and select the right products and speeds for your network.

- Chapter Five: This fabric architecture chapter looks at different solutions for the connectivity of products, their management, and how they move data across the data center.

- Chapter Six: This chapter on IP Fabrics and BGP covers how switches talk and transport traffic to each other. This connects to IP Clos networks, where the protocol selection is a manual implementation, whereas in Ethernet fabrics the vendor has done this for you. This chapter also ties back to Chapter 5 on fabric solutions.

- Chapter Seven: Overlay networking focuses on the different types of overlays supported, how they interact with the underlay networking you may have just designed, and any considerations you might take into account. This chapter looks at VTEPs, how and where they terminate, and the different types you can support.

- Chapter Eight: This chapter on controller and controller-less networks examines the benefits of using either a single pane of glass or a static-based environment for both the network and the servers, and explores whether or not there is a middle ground using popular vendor offerings.

- Chapter Nine: This chapter further explores a static-based solution for overlay networks through the use of Ethernet VPN (EVPN) to support Layer 2 overlay within the data center fabric.

Again, this book tries to simplify a complex networking entity – so use the links provided to update the precise specifications of the components, protocols, controllers, and configurations. A good place to start is at the Juniper TechLibrary: http://www.juniper.net/documentation.

The author and editors worked hard to make this data center primer nice and simple. It's a difficult thing to do, whether publishing or network architecting. Three words – *nice and simple* – should be the overriding basis of your design, no matter which Juniper technology or service you use.

By the end of this book, you should be able to explain your data center design within a few sentences. If you can't, then it's probably too complex of a design.

Colin Wrightson, October 2016

Chapter 1

Common Components

The first question to pose in any data center design is *What switch should I use and where?* Juniper Networks, like other vendors, produces data center switches that meet stringent specifications in order to fit within particular segments of a network. This chapter provides an overview of the Juniper Networks switching solution, allowing you to understand and compare the different port densities, form factors, and port capabilities of the devices. The book then moves on explain the placement of devices in the network and the different architectures they support.

NOTE   The architecture and different layers within a data center are described in more detail in subsequent chapters.

Switches Used In the Data Center

The QFX Series by Juniper Networks is specifically designed for the data center. These switches address the need for low latency and high availability, high port density, and the flexibility to support different architectures. They are ideal data center switches, and at the time of this writing, consist of the following product line: the QFX5100 Series, the QFX5200 Series, and the QFX10000 Series.

NOTE   Download each product's datasheet for up-to-date improvements and modifications made after this book was published at http://www.juniper.net/us/en/products-services/switching/qfx-series/.

MORE?   For more detailed information about Junos Fusion and data centers, see the Juniper Networks O'Reilly book, *The QFX10000 Series*, by Doug Hanks: http://www.juniper.net/us/en/training/jnbooks/oreilly-juniper-library/qfx10000-series/.

The QFX5100 Series

The QFX5100 Series has five iterations, depending on the number and type of ports each has, to meet various data center requirements.

QFX5100-48S

The QFX5100-48S is a 10-Gigabit Ethernet Enhanced Small Form-Factor Pluggable (SFP+) top-of-rack switch with 48 SFP+ ports and six Quad SFP+ (QSFP+) 40GbE ports. Each SFP+ port can operate as a native 10 Gigabit port or a 100MB/1 Gigabit port when 1_Gigabit optics are inserted. Each QSFP+ port can operate as either 40GbE uplink ports or access ports. Each QSFP port can also operate as 4x 10GbE ports using a 4x 10 breakout cable. The QFX5100-48S provides full duplex throughput of 1.44 Tbps, has a 1 U form factor, and comes standard with redundant fans and redundant power supplies. The switch is availiable with either back-to-front or front-to-back airflow and with AC or DC power supplies. The QFX5100-48S can be used in multiple architectures, such as:

- A standalone switch
- A spine or leaf in an IP Fabric (covered in later chapters)
- A master, backup, or line card in a QFX Virtual Chassis (covered later)
- A spine or leaf device in a Virtual Chassis Fabric (VCF) (covered later)
- A satellite device in a Junos Fusion fabric (covered later)

QFX5100-48T

The QFX5100-48T is a tri-speed 100/1000/10Gb BASE-T top-of-rack switch with 48 10GBASE-T access ports and six 40GbE QSFP+ ports. Each QSFP+ port can operate as either an uplink port or an access port. Each QSFP port can also operate as a 4x 10GbE port using a 4x 10 breakout cable. The QFX5100-48T provides full duplex throughput of 1.44 Tbps, has a 1 U form factor, and comes standard with redundant fans and redundant power supplies. The QFX5100-48T can be used in multiple architectures, such as:

- A standalone switch
- Leaf in a IP Fabric
- A master, backup, or line card in a QFX Virtual Chassis
- A leaf device in a VCF
- A satellite device in a Junos Fusion fabric

QFX5100-24Q

The QFX5100-24Q is a 40-Gigabit Ethernet QSFP+ switch with 24 QSFP+ ports. Each QSFP+ port can operate as a native 40 Gbps port or as four independent 10 Gbps ports. It has a 1RU form factor and comes standard with redundant fans and redundant power supplies, and can be ordered with either front-to-back or back-to-front airflow with AC or DC power supplies. The QFX5100-24Q switch also has two module bays for the optional expansion module, QFX-EM-4Q, which can add a total of eight additional QSFP+ ports to the chassis, thus providing 32 ports of 40GbE or 104 logical ports when using 10G port breakout cables. All ports on the QFX5100-24Q and QFX-EM-4Q can be configured as either access ports or as uplinks, and the QFX5100-24Q switch provides full duplex throughput of 2.56 Tbps. The QFX5100-24Q can be used in multiple architectures, such as:

- A standalone switch
- Spine or leaf in a IP Fabric
- A master, backup, or line card in a QFX Virtual Chassis
- A spine or leaf device in a VCF
- A satellite device in a Junos Fusion fabric

QFX5100-96S

The QFX5100-96S is a 10-Gigabit Ethernet Enhanced Small Form-Factor Pluggable (SFP+) top-of-rack switch with 96 SFP+ ports and eight 40GbE Quad SFP+ (QSFP+) ports. Each SFP+ port can operate as a native 10 Gbps port or as a 100MB/1 Gbps port. The eight QSFP+ ports can operate at native 40 Gbps speed or can be channelized into four independent 10 Gbps port speeds taking the total number of 10GbE ports on the switch to 128. The QFX5100-96S switch has a 2 U form factor and comes as standard with redundant fans, redundant power supplies, both AC or DC power support, and the option of either front-to-back or back-to-front airflow. The QFX5100-96S can be used in multiple architectures, such as:

- A standalone switch
- Spine or leaf in a IP Fabric
- A member of a QFX Virtual Chassis
- A spine or leaf device in a VCF
- A satellite device in a Junos Fusion fabric

QFX5100-24Q-AA

The QFX5100-24Q-AA is the same as the QFX5100-24Q with 24 QSFP+ ports of 40-Gigabit Ethernet. Each QSFP+ port can operate as a native 40 Gbps port or as four independent 10 Gbps ports. It has a 1RU form factor and comes standard with redundant fans, redundant power supplies, and can be ordered with either front-to-back or back-to-front airflow with AC or DC power supplies. The QFX5100-24Q switch provides full duplex throughput of 2.56 Tbps. The QFX5100-24Q-AA module bay can accommodate a single Packet Flow Accelerator (PFA), a doublewide expansion module (QFX-PFA-4Q), or two singlewide optional expansion modules as the standard QFX5100-24Q.

The QFX-PFA-4Q, which features a high-performance field-programmable gate array (FPGA), provides four additional QSFP+ ports to the chassis. This switch provides the hardware support to enable Precision Time Protocol (PTP) boundary clocks by using the QFX-PFA-4Q module. The QFX5100-24Q-AA also supports GPS or PPS in and out signals when QFX-PFA-4Q is installed.

The CPU subsystem of this switch includes a two-port 10-Gigabit Ethernet network interface card (NIC) to provide a high bandwidth path or to alternate traffic path to guest VMs directly from the Packet Forwarding Engine.

The QFX5100-24Q-AA can be used as a standalone switch that supports high frequency statistics collection. Working with the Juniper Networks Cloud Analytics Engine, this switch monitors and reports the workload and application behavior across the physical and virtual infrastructure.

The QFX5100-24Q-AA can be used as a top-of-rack switch where you need application processing in the switch or Layer 4 services such as NAT (Network Address Translation), packet encryption, load balancing, and many more services.

MORE? The data sheets and other information for all of the QFX5100 Series outlined above can be found at http://www.juniper.net/assets/us/en/local/pdf/datasheets/1000480-en.pdf.

The QFX5200 Series

At the time of this book's publication, the QFX5200 Series is comprised of a single device, the 32C.

QFX5200-32C

The QFX5200-32C is a 100 Gigabit Ethernet top-of-rack switch that supports 10/25/40/50 and 100GbE connectivity, allowing this 1RU switch to support the following port configurations:

- 32 ports of 100GbE
- 32 ports of 40GbE
- 64 ports of 50GbE (using a breakout cable)
- 128 ports of 25GbE (using a breakout cable)
- 128 ports of 10GbE (using a breakout cable)

The QFX5200-32C comes standard with redundant fans and redundant power supplies supporting either AC or DC, and is available with either front–to-back or back-to-front airflow. The QFX5200 can be used in multiple architectures, such as:

- A standalone switch
- Spine or leaf in a IP Fabric
- A satellite device in a Junos Fusion fabric

MORE?   The datasheets and other information for all of the QFX5200 Series outlined above can be found at http://www.juniper.net/us/en/products-services/switching/qfx-series/

The QFX10000 Series

The QFX10000 Series is comprised of four platforms at the time of this book's publication: the fixed format QFX10002-36Q and QFX10002-72Q, and the chassis-based QFX10008 and QFX10016.

QFX10002-36Q

The QFX10002-36Q is a 100 Gigabit Ethernet aggregation and spine layer switch that supports 10/40 and 100GbE connectivity, allowing this 2RU switch to support the following port configurations:

- 12 ports of 100GbE
- 36 ports of 40GbE
- 144 ports of 10GbE (using a breakout cable)

The QFX10002-36Q comes standard with redundant fans and redundant power supplies supporting either AC or DC, and can be ordered with front-to-back airflow. The QFX10002-36Q series and can be used in multiple architectures, such as:

- A standalone switch
- Leaf or spine layer switch in a IP Fabric
- A aggregation device in a Junos Fusion fabric

QFX10002-72Q

The QFX10002-72Q is a 100 Gigabit Ethernet aggregation and spine layer switch that supports 10/40 and 100GbE connectivity. Allowing this 2RU switch supports the following port configurations:

- 24 ports of 100GbE
- 72 ports of 40GbE
- 288 ports of 10GbE (using a breakout cable)

The QFX10002-72Q comes standard with redundant fans and redundant power supplies supporting either AC or DC, and can be ordered with front-to-back airflow. The QFX10002-72Q series can be used in multiple architectures, such as:

- A standalone switch
- Leaf or spine layer switch in a IP Fabric
- A aggregation device in a Junos Fusion fabric

MORE?   Complete, up-to-date details on the two fixed QFX10000 Series switches can found here: http://www.juniper.net/assets/us/en/local/pdf/datasheets/1000529-en.pdf.

QFX10008

The QFX10008 is a chassis-based high-density aggregation and spine layer switch that supports 1/10/40 and 100GbE connectivity across eight slots, allowing this 13RU switch to support the following port configurations:

- 240 ports of 100GbE
- 288 ports of 40GbE
- 1152 ports of 10GbE

The QFX10008 supports three line card options:

- The QFX10000-36Q line card provides 36 ports of 40GbE, 12 ports of 100GbE, and 144 ports of 10GbE with breakout cables
- The QFX10000-30C line card provides 30 ports of 40GbE and 30 ports of 100GbE
- The QFX10000-60S-6Q line card provides 60 ports of 1/10GbE with six ports of 40GbE and 2 ports of 100GbE

The QFX10008 comes standard with redundant route engines (supervisor cards in Cisco speak) in a mid-planeless architecture that supports dual redundant fan trays, with six redundant power supplies supporting either AC or DC, and can be ordered with front-to-back or back-to-front airflow. The QFX10008 series can be used in multiple architectures, such as:

- A standalone switch
- Leaf, spine, or aggregation layer switch in a IP Fabric (covered in later sections)
- A aggregation device in a Junos Fusion fabric (covered in later sections)

QFX10016

The QFX10016 is a chassis-based aggregation and spine layer switch that supports 10/40 and 100GbE connectivity across 16 slots. This 21RU switch supports the following port configurations:

- 480 ports of 100GbE
- 576 ports of 40GbE
- 2304 ports of 10GbE

The QFX10016 supports three line card options:

- The QFX10000-36Q line card provides 36 ports of 40GbE, 12 ports of 100GbE, and 144 ports of 10GbE
- The QFX10000-30C line card provides 30 ports of 40GbE and 30 ports of 100GbE
- The QFX10000-60S-6Q line card provides 84 ports of 10GbE, six ports of 40GbE, and two ports of 100GbE

The QFX10016 comes standard with redundant route engines in a mid-planeless architecture that supoprts dual redundant fan trays, with ten redundant power supplies supporting either AC or DC, and can be ordered with front-to-back airflow. The QFX10016 series can be used in multiple architectures, such as:

- A standalone switch
- Leaf, spine, or aggregation layer switch in a IP Fabric (covered in later sections)
- A aggregation device in a Junos Fusion fabric (covered in later sections)

MORE?   Up-to-date details on the chassis-based QFX10000 series switches can found here: http://www.juniper.net/assets/us/en/local/pdf/datasheets/1000529-en.pdf.

MORE?   For more detailed information about the QFX Series and data centers, see the Juniper/O'Reilly book, *The QFX10000 Series*, at http://www.juniper.net/books.

With so many iterations of the QFX Series, it's worth discussing the different silicon types used in these products as it can have a bearing on their placement in the data center and their capabilities once installed.

Custom and Merchant Silicon

When silicon is discussed in this book, it means the Packet Forwarding Engine or ASIC (application-specific integrated circuit) that a switch uses to process L2 packets. *Merchant silicon* describes the use of "off the shelf" third-party Packet Forwarding Engines that can be implemented into a networking product, whereas *custom silicon* relates to a company, like Juniper, that designs their own Packet Forwarding Engines and implements them into their own products.

Merchant silicon is used throughout the industry by multiple switch vendors and for good reason – it's an efficient method of bringing new switches and capabilities to market in a shorter timeframe than a custom silicon product. But there are always trade-offs to consider with a mass-market product.

For example, the QFX5100 and 5200 Series devices both use Broadcom Packet Forwarding Engines. Specifically, the QFX5100 uses the Broadcom T2 chipset and the QFX5200 uses the newer Broadcom Tomahawk Chipset. This is no different than Cisco, Arista, HP, Dell Force 10, Huawei, and others who use Broadcom in their versions of similar switches.

These are excellent switches with high throughput, high port densities, and with a software feature set that provides 90% of what most networks need to do with a switching device. But the trade-off is that these are generic devices that have a low buffer capability, a default set of features that may not be able to be enhanced outside of the parameters that are supported in that hardware, and, given how fast these products come to market, they could be out of date very quickly.

The other option is to use a product based on custom silicon, with a chipset such as the one found in the QFX10000 Series. With custom-made silicon, you'll get a higher level of innovation that will allow scaling and newer services to be introduced in software rather than hardware. This in turn will allow you to be more flexible in supporting a greater number of different port speeds and other hardware-related features, higher buffer capabilities, and a more flexible software feature set allowing it to be placed at different areas of the network.

But the trade- off is that custom silicon products will be more expensive due to the higher level of investment and research that has gone into their development. This means the product will be on the market longer than a merchant silicon version (to recoup the initial production costs) and that you need to consider future technology shifts that may happen and their effects on both types of products.

There are pros and cons to both approaches, so I suggest you consider using both merchant and custom silicon, but in different positions within the network to get the best results.

Network designers tend to use the following rule of thumb: use merchant silicon at the leaf/server layer where the Layer 2 and Layer 3 throughput and latency is the main requirement, with minimal buffers, higher port densities, support for open standards, and innovation in the switches OS software. Then, at the spine or core, where all the traffic is aggregated, custom silicon should be used, as the benefits are greater bandwidth, port density, and larger buffers. You can also implement more intelligence at the spine or core to allow for other protocols such as EVPN for Data Center Interconnect (DCI), analytics engines, and other NFV-based products that may need more resources than are provided on a merchant silicon-based switch.

IMPORTANT   The most important aspect in this requirement is making sure the products you have selected have all the required features and performance capabilities for the applications you need. *Always seek out the most current specifications, datasheets, and up-to-date improvements on the vendor's web site.* For up-to-date information about Juniper switching platforms, you can go to: http://www.juniper.net/us/en/products-services/switching/.

Chapter 2

Architectures

Now that you have a better understanding of the Juniper products for the data center, let's move on to the different types of physical architectures that can be deployed. The physical architecture is defined as the physical placement of your switches in relation to the physical rack deployment in the data center you are either considering or have already implemented.

There are two main deployment designs, either *top-of-rack* or *end-of-row*.

Top-of-Rack

In top-of-rack (ToR) designs one or two Ethernet switches are installed inside each rack to provide local server connectivity. While the name *top-of-rack* would imply placement of the switch at the top of the physical rack, in reality the switch placement can be at the bottom or middle of the rack (top-of-rack typically provides an easier point of access and cable management to the switch).

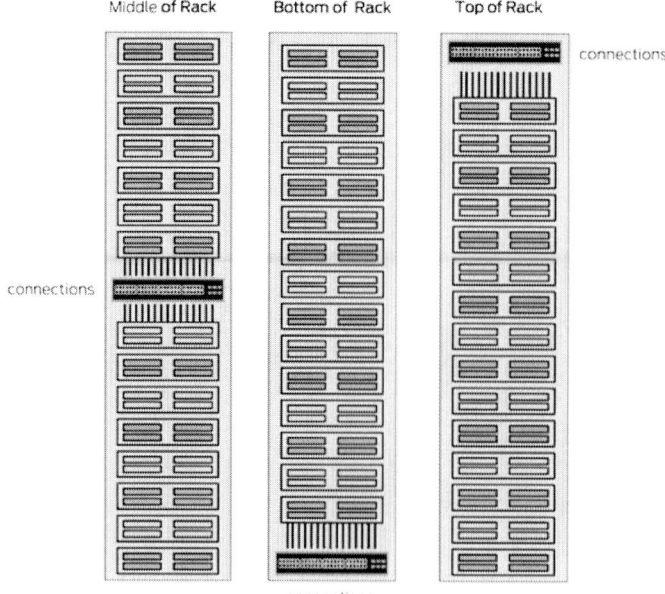

Figure 2.1   ToR Switch Positions

The switches deployed at the top-of-rack are typically of a fixed format, 1RU to 2RU in height. The QFX5100, QFX5110 and QFX5200 switches are examples of switches developed for this requirement.

The main benefit of positioning your switches within racks is the ease of server-to-switch connectivity, removing the need for long cable runs, while allowing 1GbE copper, and 10 or 40GbE fiber/DAC cables to be run directly from the servers to the switch. This style of implementation eliminates the need for cabling patch panels, which requires additional racks, and running large quantities of cabling between racks. Top-of-rack eliminates the issues around long cable runs and makes replacing cables easier when faster network speeds are required.

With a top-of-rack design, each rack can be managed as a single entity within the data center. This can make the process of server swaps and upgrades easier because they can be implemented on a rack-by-rack basis without affecting other servers and related applications in other racks. It also means that upgrades on the switches can be done in a managed and staged approach, whereby once the top switches are upgraded first and traffic is again flowing, the secondary switch in the rack can be upgraded and so on. The implementation of in-service software upgrades (ISSU) in top-of-rack switches removes this need altogether, but as you'll see in Chapter 5 on fabric architecture, there are usually some caveats.

Connectivity from the top-of-rack switch to the aggregation layer is usually via dual 10 or 40GbE fiber connections for resiliency, as shown below in Figure 2.2.

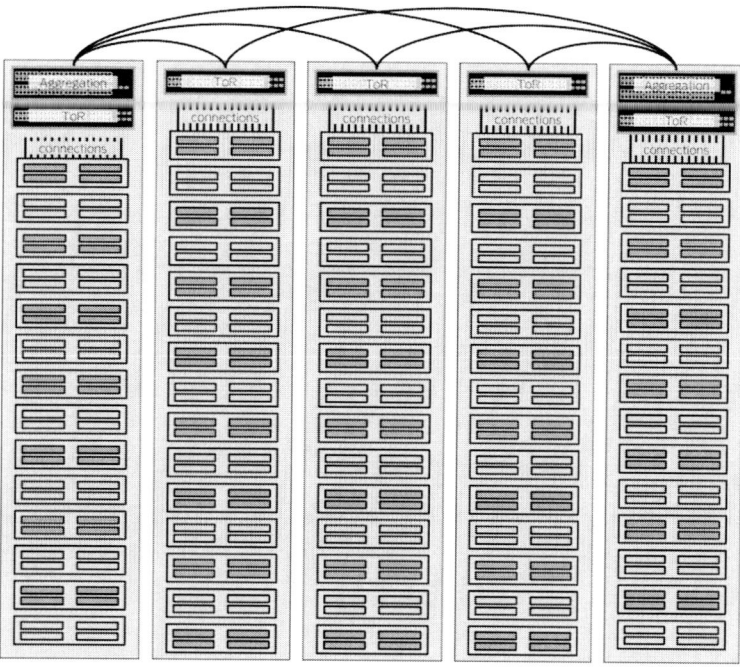

Figure 2.2   **ToR to Aggregation Uplinks**

For uplink cables, fiber provides a considerably better investment for long-term deployments than copper cabling, as it can carry higher bandwidths over a longer distance and provide the flexibility to support higher bandwidth when higher speeds are required.

With this in mind the top-of-rack switch you select should be able to support flexible uplink port speeds. An example would be the QFX5100-48S, which has six 40GbE uplink ports, but each of those uplink ports can be broken down into four individual 10GbE links. So while your requirements on day one may only be for 10GbE uplinks, you know you have the ability to support 40GbE in the future without the need to swap out expensive hardware.

Arguably, one of the disadvantages of the top-of-rack design is the expansion in size of your management domain, as every switch is an individually managed device with all of the configuration and software burdens that come with that device. For example, if you have a data center with ten rows of ten racks, with two switches per rack, that's 200 switches that need to be managed and monitored. While a lot of the configuration can be duplicated for the majority of switches, that still represents a lot of overhead from a management point of view and exposes many potential points in the network to misconfiguration.

NOTE   Juniper has addressed these concerns by providing virtualization technologies like Virtual Chassis Fabric and Junos Fusion to simplify the management domain. This simplification is achieved by implementing a virtualized control plane over a large number of switches, effectively creating a large virtual switch where each physical switch is a virtual line card. You then have the flexibility to implement your virtual switch over several racks, or rows of racks, and provide faster implementation with a single point of configuration over virtual pods or clusters of network switches. These technologies are discussed in more detail in Chapter 5 of this book: *Fabric Architecture*.

Another disadvantage in top-of-rack design is in the number of ports you might waste. The average top-of-rack switch comes with 48 ports of 1/10GbE. With two switches per rack, that provides 96 ports per rack. You would need a lot of servers per rack to utilize all of those connections. This is where an end-of-row solution provides an advantage as you waste fewer ports but increase the number and size of inter-rack cable connections.

There are ways around the port wastage, such as cross connecting servers between racks. While not a great idea from a cable management point of view, cross connecting does allow you to better utilize your switch ports and provide resiliency for servers. As the diagram in Figure 2.3 illustrates, a 48-port switch would be positioned in each rack, 24 ports are dedicated to the servers in that rack and the other 24 are dedicated for the rack next to it.

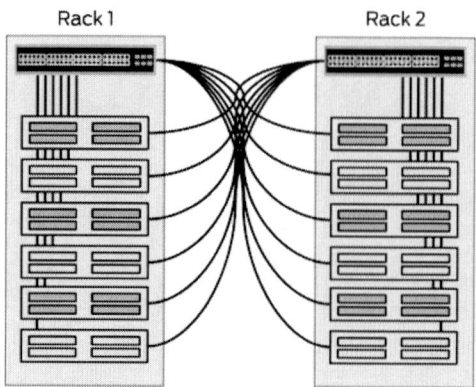

Figure 2.3   **ToR Cross Connect**

In the other rack the same is done again and 50% of the server connections cross into the other rack and vise versa. As mentioned earlier, this is not the most elegant of designs, and you would need to factor in extra cable length to bridge the gap between racks, but it is more practical and less expensive than a two switch per rack design.

And this situation brings up a good point: not every data center installation or design is perfect, so if the last example works for you and you are aware of its limitations and potential issues, then implement accordingly.

Table 2.1   Summary of ToR Design

Advantages	Limitations
Cabling complexity is reduced as all the servers are connected to the switches located in the same rack and only fiber uplink connections pass outside the rack.	There may be more unused ports in each rack and it is very difficult to accurately provide the required number of ports. This results in higher un-utilized ports/ power/ cooling.
If the racks are small, there could be one network switch for two-three racks.	Unplanned Expansions (within a rack) might be difficult to achieve using the ToR approach.
ToR architecture supports modular deployment of data center racks as each rack can come in-built with all the necessary cabling/ switches and can be deployed quickly on-site.	Each switch needs to be managed independently. So your CapEx and OpEx costs might be higher in ToR deployments.
This design provides scalability, because you may require 1GE/ 10GE today, but you can upgrade to 10GE/ 40GE in the future with minimum costs and changes to cabling.	1U/2U switches are used in each rack, achieving scalability beyond a certain number of ports would become difficult.

End-of-Row

The end-of-row design (EoR) was devised to provide two central points of aggregation for server connectivity in a row of cabinets as opposed to aggregation within each rack as shown in the top-of-rack design. Each server within each cabinet would be connected to each end-of-row switch cabinet either directly via RJ45, via fiber, or if the length is not too great, with DAC or via a patch panel present in each rack.

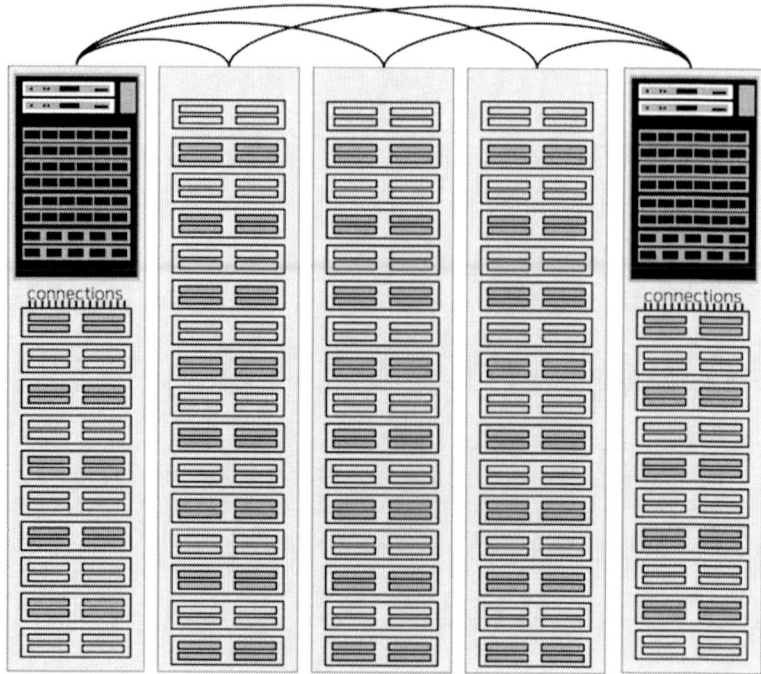

Figure 2.4   **EoR Design**

For a redundant design there might be two bundles of cables to each rack, each running to opposite end-of-row network racks. Within the server rack the bundle of cable is normally wired to one or more patch panels fixed to the top of the cabinet

The individual servers use a relatively short RJ45/DAC/Fiber patch cable to connect from the server to the patch panel in the same rack. The bundles of cable from each rack can then be channeled through either overhead cable troughs or under floor bundles to the end-of-row network racks. Depending on how much cabling is required, it's common to have a rack dedicated to patching all of the adjacent cables, or within the rack that contains the end-of-row network switch.

It is also quite common to directly connect the server cables to the end-of-row switches as opposed to via a patch panel, but again this is dependent on your cabling policy, distance, and cable bundle sizes.

Another version of this design is referred to as middle-of-row which involves bundles of cables from each server rack going to a pair of racks positioned in the middle of the row. Both designs are valid but careful consideration needs to be taken concerning the cabling design for either design can end up in a mess.

The switch positioned in either the end-of-row or middle-of-row is generally a chassis based model. A chassis based switch would provide a higher density of network connections and possibly a higher level of availability, as the chassis would have multiple power supplies, dual routing engines, and multiple fabric cards. This is the case with most chassis-based solutions from Juniper – if you need faster connection rates then all you need to do is upgrade the physical line cards in the device, not the whole chassis, allowing core components to last a lot longer than a typical top-of-rack switch at a lower OPEX cost over the lifetime of the device.

From a management point of view, your management domain is considerably reduced because it is based on an entire row rather than the top-of-rack design where your domain is per rack. However, it does mean that your failure domain increases to encompass all of the servers in that row, and that upgrades need to be better planned because the effect of a failure would have a larger impact than you have in the top-of-rack design (and it removes the top-of-rack option to upgrade certain racks based on common applications or services).

One benefit, which is discussed in Chapter 4, is that your over-subscription ratios or contention ratios will be potentially better in an end-of-row design as compared to a top-of-rack design. For example, what if you were terminating 48 ports of 10GbE per line card and you wanted to keep a 3:1 ratio of server to uplink traffic? Several years ago this would involve terminating all of your 10GbE connections over several line cards and then pushing this traffic to the backplane and a dedicated uplink line card. You would have had to provision 160GbE of uplink capacity, or 4x 40GbE, to hit that ratio and then it would only have been for those 48 ports. If you need to terminate more than that number of 10GbE connections you would need more than 40GbE.

Today, with mixed speed line cards, you can use a 60x 10GbE line card that also has an additional 6x 40GbE or 2x 100GbE, allowing you to hit a lower contention ratio on the same card without sending traffic via the backplane, and that's traffic dedicated to that line card, which means you can replicate it over every line card.

Table 2.2   Summary of EoR Design

Advantages	Limitations
Since Chassis Switches are deployed in EoR configurations, expansion (for the total number of ports) can be done by just adding a line card as most of the Chassis Switches are planned for expandable configurations, without limiting backplane capacities.	The EoR architecture would bring down the number of un-utilized switch ports, drastically. This decreases the capital expenditure, running costs, and time needed for maintenance.
Chassis Switches enable a high availability configuration with almost no single points of failure, as most of the critical components (control module, cooling module, power supply module, etc.) can be deployed in redundant (1+1 or N+1 or N+N) configurations. The failover is almost immediate (often without affecting end user sessions).	Longer cables are required to connect the Chassis switch (at end of the row) to each server, in EoR deployments and hence special arrangements might be required to carry them over to the aggregation switch. This might result in excessive space utilization at the rack/ data center cabling routes, increasing the amount of data center space required to store the same number of servers.
Placement of servers can be decided independently, without any 'minimum/maximum servers in a single rack' constraints. So, servers can be placed more evenly across the racks and hence there may not be excessive cooling requirements due to densely placed servers.	Each switch needs to be managed independently. So your CapEx and OpEx costs might be higher in ToR deployments.
Since each packet fewer switches to pass through, the latency and delay involved in passing through multiple switches is minimized.	The cost of higher performance cables (used in data centers) can be considerable and hence cabling costs can get higher than ToR deployments. Also, fault finding on cabling issues (especially if cabling needs to be replaced) becomes more intrusive and adds to overall OpEx.
The EoR architecture would drastically reduce the number of switch ports that are not being utilized. This decreases the CapEx, running costs, and time needed for maintenance.	It's difficult, and more expensive, to upgrade cabling infrastructure to support higher speeds or performance, as lengthier cables need to be replaced individually when upgrading from 10GE to 40GE, for example.
Servers that exchange a considerable amount of data packets between each other can be connected to the same line card in the Chassis switch, regardless of the rack they belong to. This minimizes delay and enables better performance due to local switching.	

Chapter 3

Cabling

The last chapter on top-of-rack and end-of-row placement of the components brought to light the importance of data center physical cabling design. When designing a cabling infrastructure, the physical layout of the cabling plant, the signal attenuation and distance, as well as installation and termination, require thorough consideration. Investing in the optimal cabling media to support not only your day one requirements, but also the need for higher media speeds such as 40, and 100 Gigabit Ethernet (GbE) connectivity involves striking a balance among bandwidth, flexibility, and cost designed for your purposes.

Most component vendors provide three supported options: *copper*, *fiber*, and *direct attach copper* (DAC). Let's discuss each and how you might implement any of them into your design.

Copper

Copper cabling is often referred to as Cat5e and Cat6, which refers to RJ45 terminated cabling over a twisted pair that provides support for 10/100/1000Mb and 10GbE connection speeds over a certain frequency up to 100m. See Table 3.1 below for detailed information.

In the context of a top-of-rack design solution, one would expect copper to be implemented within each rack. In an end-of-row design solution the copper cabling could be implemented between the servers and switches, but the distance would need to be considered as well as the size of the cabling plant. Also, any future upgrades might mean removing this cabling to support higher speeds, which is always a consideration.

But if this is what's required, then the QFX5100 series supports it in the form of the QFX5100-48T switch. You also have the option of using the EX4300 and EX3400 series.

Table 3.1 provides an overview of the different connector types, cable standards, cabling, distances each cable can cover, the frequency typically used, and where in the design the cable is used, as well as the Juniper Networks supported switch series, the EX or QFX Series.

Table 3.1   Copper Cabling Options

Connector/ Media	IEEE Cable Standard	Max Distance	Frequency (MHz)	Recommended Placement and Supported Switch
1000BASE-T Copper	CAT 5e CAT 6 CAT 6A (STP/UTP)	328 ft (100 m)	1-100 1-250 1-500	ToR in rack QFX5100-48T EX4300 and EX3400
100BASE-TX	CAT 5e CAT 6 CAT 6A (STP/UTP)	328 ft (100 m)	1-100 1-250 1-500	ToR in rack QFX5100-48T EX4300 and EX3400
10GBASE-T	CAT 7	328 ft (100 m)	1–600	ToR in rack QFX5100-48T
	CAT 6A	328 ft (100 m)	1–500	
	CAT 6 (UTP)	98 ft (30 m)	1–250	
	CAT 6 (STP)	98 ft (30 m)	1–250	

Fiber

There are two classifications for optical fiber: *single-mode fiber-optic* (SMF) and *multimode fiber-optic* (MMF).

In SMF, light follows a single path through the fiber while in MMF it takes multiple paths resulting in a differential mode delay or (DMD).

In the context of a top-of-rack design solution one would expect MMF to be used within each rack and between connecting racks up to the aggregation layer, if the distance is relatively short (up to 400m). In an end-of-row design solution it could be implemented between the servers and switches. If distance permits, then MMF could also be implemented up to a core or aggregation layer, and if not, then then you could implement SMF.

All of the switches in the QFX Series support fiber interfaces. To make things a little easier Table 3.2 lists an overview of the different connector types, cable standards, cabling types, the distances each can cover, the wavelengths used, where in the design the cable is used, and the Juniper Networks supported switch series.

Table 3.2   **Fiber Cabling Options**

Connector/ Media	IEEE Cable Standard	Fiber Grade & Max Distance	Wavelength	Recommended Placement and Supported Switch
1000BASE-T RJ45 Copper SFP	RJ-45	328 ft (100 m)		ToR in rack QFX5100-48S & 96T
1000BASE-SX	LC-MMF	FDDI - 220m (721 ft) OM1 - 275m (902 ft) 500m (1640 ft) OM2 - 550m (1804 ft)	1-160 1-200 1-400 1-500	ToR & EoR QFX5100 & EX Series
1000BASE-LX	LC – SMF	SMF – 10Km (6.2m) OM1 – 550m (1804 ft) 500m (1640 ft) OM2 - 550m (1804 ft)	1-500 1-400 1-500	ToR & EoR within rack QFX5100 Series
10G-USR	LC- MMF	OM1 – 10m (32 ft) OM2 – 30m (98 ft) OM3 – 100m (328 ft)	840 nm to 860 nm	ToR & EoR in & out of rack QFX5100 & QFX10000 Series

Standard	Connector/Fiber	Distance	Wavelength	Usage
10GBASE-SR	LC-MMF	FDDI – 26m (85 ft) OM1 - 33m (108 ft) 66m (216 ft) OM2 - 82m (269 ft) OM3 - 300m (984 ft) OM4 – 400m (1213 ft)	840 nm to 860 nm	ToR & EoR for both in rack and out of rack. QFX5100 & QFX10000 Series
10GBASE-LR	LC – SMF	10km (6.2 miles)	1260 nm to 1355 nm	ToR & EoR out of rack QFX5100 & QFX10000 Series
10GBASE-ER	LC-SMF	40km (24.85 miles)	1530 nm to 1565 nm	Long Distance DCI
40GBASE-SR4	12-ribbon multimode fiber crossover cable – MMF	OM3 - 100m (325 ft) OM4 – 150m (425 ft)	840 nm to 860 nm	ToR & EoR out of rack QFX5100 & QFX10000 Series
40GX10G-ESR4	12-ribbon multimode fiber crossover cable - MMF	OM3 - 300m (984 ft) OM4 – 400m (1312 ft)	840 nm to 860 nm	ToR & EoR out of rack QFX5100 & QFX10000 Series
40GBASE-LR4	LC – SMF	10 Km (6.2 miles)	See note *	ToR & EoR out of rack QFX5100 & QFX10000 Series
40G-LX4	Dual LC – SMF & MMF	OS1 – 2 KM OM3 – 100m (328 ft) OM4 – 150m (492 ft)	See note *	ToR & EoR out of rack QFX5100 & QFX10000 Series
40G-IR4	LC – SMF	2 Km (1.24 miles)	See note *	ToR & EoR out of rack QFX5100 & QFX10000 Series
100GBASE-SR4	12-ribbon multimode fiber crossover cable – MMF	OM3 – 70m (230 ft) OM4 – 100m (325 ft)	840 nm to 860 nm	ToR & EoR out of rack QFX10000 Series
100GBASE-LR4	LC or Dual LC – SMF	10 Km (6.2 miles)	See note *	ToR & EoR out of rack QFX10000 Series

*TABLE 3.2 NOTE These wavelengths refer to a wavelength range that varies depending on which lane is used. Please refer to the following link for more details from Juniper Networks: http://www.juniper.net/techpubs/en_US/release-independent/junos/topics/reference/specifications/optical-interface-qsfp28-qfx.html.

DAC or Twinax

DAC or Twinax cabling is a copper cable that comes in either *active* or *passive assembly* and connects directly in to a SFP+ (small form-factor pluggable plus) or QSFP+ (quad small form-factor plus) covering. An active DAC cable has amplification and equalization built into the cable assembly to improve the signal quality, while a passive DAC cable has a straight wire with no signal amplification built into the cable assembly. In most cases a rule of thumb is that for distances shorter than 5 meters you go with a passive DAC, and greater than 5 meters with an active DAC.

Due to its low cost, in comparison to fiber, DAC makes perfect sense for short runs inside the rack in a top-of-rack solution, and if the distance between racks is less than 10 meters, between racks in a end-of-row solution as well.

The SFP+ DAC cable allows for a serial data transmission up to 10.3Gb/s, which is a low cost choice for very short reach applications of 10GbE or 1-8G Fiber Channel.

QSFP+ 40GbE DAC allows for bidirectional data transmission up to 40GbE over four lanes of twin-axial cable, delivering serialized data at a rate of 10.3125 Gbit/s per lane.

QSFP+ 100GbE DAC cable allows for bidirectional data transmission up to 100GbE over four lanes of twin-axial cable, delivering serialized data at a rate of 28 Gbit/s per lane.

Table 3.3 outlines the different types of DAC cables you can use in a data center. This table differs from the preceding tables on copper and fiber cabling because it includes the bend radius. The bend radius is an important point to keep in mind because like many cables, these cables are sensitive to adverse bending, which can effect data rates.

Table 3.3 DAC Cabling Options

Connector/Media	IEEE Cable Standard	Max Distance	Minimum Cable Bend Radius	Recommended Placement and Supported Switch
QFX-SFP-DAC-1M – 10GbE	SFP permanently attached.	1 m (3.3 ft)	1 in. (2.54 cm)	ToR in rack QFX5100 & QFX10000 Series
QFX-SFP-DAC-2M – 10GbE	SFP permanently attached.	2 m (6.6 ft)	1 in. (2.54 cm)	ToR in rack QFX5100 & QFX10000 Series
QFX-SFP-DAC-3M – 10GbE	SFP permanently attached.	3 m (9.9 ft)	1 in. (2.54 cm)	ToR in rack QFX5100 & QFX10000 Series

QFX-SFP-DAC-5M – 10GbE	SFP permanently attached.	5 m (16.4 ft)	1 in. (2.54 cm)	ToR in rack QFX5100 & QFX10000 Series
QFX-SFP-DAC-7MA – 10GbE	SFP permanently attached.	7 m (23 ft)	1 in. (2.54 cm)	ToR in rack QFX5100 & QFX10000 Series
QFX-SFP-DAC-10MA – 10GbE	SFP permanently attached.	10 m (32.8 ft)	1 in. (2.54 cm)	ToR in rack QFX5100 & QFX10000 Series
QFX-QSFP-DAC-1M – 40GbE	SFP permanently attached.	1 m (3.3 ft)	1 in. (2.54 cm)	ToR in rack QFX5100 & QFX10000 Series
QFX-QSFP-DAC-3M – 40GbE	SFP permanently attached.	3 m (9.9 ft)	1 in. (2.54 cm)	ToR in rack QFX5100 & QFX10000 Series
QFX-QSFP-DAC-5M – 40GbE	SFP permanently attached.	5 m (16.4 ft)	1 in. (2.54 cm)	ToR in rack QFX5100 & QFX10000 Series
QFX-QSFP-DAC-7MA – 40GbE	SFP permanently attached.	7 m (22.9 ft)	1 in. (2.54 cm)	ToR in rack QFX5100 & QFX10000 Series
QFX-QSFP-DAC-10MA – 40GbE	SFP permanently attached.	10 m (32.8 ft)	1 in. (2.54 cm)	ToR in rack QFX5100 & QFX10000 Series
QFX-QSFP28-DAC-1M – 100GbE	SFP permanently attached.	1 m (3.3 ft)	1 in. (2.54 cm)	ToR in rack QFX5200 & QFX10000 Series
QFX-QSFP28-DAC-3M – 100GbE	SFP permanently attached.	3 m (9.9 ft)	4.9 cm (1.93 in.)	ToR in rack QFX5200 & QFX10000 Series

There are also a few other choices of cable types at 40GbE, including Active Optical Cables, which can go up to 30 meters and can provide for another option in both top-of-rack and end-of-row solutions. Another solution, if you don't require 40GbE on day one, is to use 40GbE to 4x 10GbE breakout cables. These allow you to break a native 40GbE interface into 4x 10GbE SFP or DAC interfaces.

If there were a best practice design, then it would be as simple as DAC/Active Optical Cables and RJ45 within racks, and fiber between racks.

MORE?   Details on the cables supported for all of the QFX products mentioned in this chapter can be found here: http://pathfinder.juniper.net/hct/category/catKey=100001&pf=QFX+Series&standard=Ethernet.º

Chapter 4

Oversubscription

This *Day One* book defines *oversubscription* as the maximum throughput of all active southbound connections divided by the maximum throughput of the northbound connections, or, in plain language, if you have 20 servers each running at 10GbE connecting to a single switch, that's 200GbE in combined (southbound) connectivity. If you have 2x 40GbE uplink connections to the next layer in the network on the same switch, that's 80GbE of northbound connectivity (200 divided by 80 equals 2.5). So 2.5 is the oversubscription ratio.

Some people (generally server teams) may see this as a failure of the network (not being able to provision 1:1), but servers rarely run at 100% bandwidth, so an element of oversubscription is fine and is often required, unless money is no object. Working with your server and application teams to define an acceptable ratio and design the network accordingly is critical to your data center design.

And that's the purpose of this chapter, to take what you have learned in the previous chapters and start applying it to this book's default design for instructional purposes.

Before moving on to that design phase, there are two more points to touch on: *switch oversubscription* and *network oversubscription*.

Switch oversubscription occurs when the overall internal switching bandwidth of the switch is less than the total bandwidth of all ingress switch ports. So, if you have a 48-port switch with every port supporting 10GbE, you would have 480GbE in switch capacity. If the internal bandwidths on the switch can only switch 240GbE of traffic at any one time, then you have a 2:1 oversubscription ratio.

While top-of-rack 1RU switches from most vendors are now line rate (Juniper switches have *always* been line rate), you do see oversubscription from the line card to the backplane on chassis-based switches in an end-of-row design. Always check the backplane switch capacity in both directions, as some vendors like to state a figure that you have to divide by two in order to get the real bandwidth.

And as described in the first paragraph of this chapter, network oversubscription refers to a point of bandwidth consolidation where the ingress or incoming bandwidth is greater than the egress or outgoing bandwidth, thus getting the oversubscription ratio to a degree that works for you and the applications you need to support.

Oversubscription Design

The starting point in designing any network is to understand the requirements that have been set and design from that point forward. To make this hypothetical as real as possible and provide a foundation for the rest of the book, let's consider the following client requirements:

The client has two *greenfield* data centers (DC1 & DC2) that are 40Km apart and will be connected to each other via the client's MPLS WAN currently running on Juniper MX Series.

DC1:

- DC1 will have five rows of 10 racks
- Each rack in DC1 will house 14 servers
- Each server has 3x 10GbE Fiber connections plus a single 1GbE RJ45 management connection
- Client would like a spine and leaf-based top-of-rack solution
- Oversubscription ratio of 4:1 or lower (lower is preferred)

DC2:

- DC2 will also have five rows of 10 racks
- Each rack in DC2 will house five blade chassis with 4x 10GbE per chassis
- Client would like an end-of-row/middle-of-row solution
- Oversubscription ratio of 1:4 or lower (lower is preferred)

Both data centers should be provisioned with support for EVPN to allow Layer 2 stretch and possible support for multi-tenancy in the future.

With these requirements outlined, let's begin to work out our subscription ratio and product placement.

DC1 Design

Starting with DC1, each rack houses 14 servers. Each server has 3x 10GbE fiber connections plus 1x 1GbE RJ45 connection for out of band (OoB).

- Total per rack = 3 x 14 (number of 10GbE times the number of servers) = 42, plus 14 x 1GbE = 14
- Total per a rack is 42 x 10GbE plus 14 x 1GbE
- Per a row – 42 x 10 (number of 10GbE per rack times the number of racks per a row) = 420
- Plus 14 x 10 (number of 1GbE times the number of racks per a row) = 140

NOTE The ratio of 10GbE and 1GbE per a row was used just in case end-of-row is offered instead of top-of-rack at DC1.

From a subscription point of view, a rack has a total bandwidth of 420 GbE. With a 4:1 subscription ratio that would be 420 / 4 (total bandwidth divided by the subscription ratio) = 105 GbE as the uplink capacity.

To hit the 105GbE mark or better you need to use 40GbE uplinks. You could go with 3 x 40GbE, which would equal 120GbE, which would lower the subscription ratio to 5:3, but this would mean *three* spine or aggregation layer switches to terminate the uplinks, which is never ideal. If you propose 4 x 40GbE per a top-of-rack switch, then you have 160GbE of uplink capacity, which would give us a subscription ratio of 2.65:1. This would also mean you could either have two, or four, spine-layer switches per row and either 2 x 40GbE per spine layer, or if we go with four spine-layer switches, then a single 40GbE connection to each.

Once you know what your interface specifications are you can match them against the available products. The QFX5100-48S provides 48 ports of 10GbE and 6 x 40GbE uplinks, so it's perfect.

NOTE At this point a good designer should ask the client about resiliency. Would a single switch per rack be okay, or would the client rather have two switches per rack, which would increase cost and waste ports? This is where an end-of-row solution could be a more cost-efficient answer, as you get both the resiliency and better port utilization. For the sake of brevity, let's assume that the client is happy with the single top-of-rack per rack and a top-of-rack-based architecture.

The rack design will look similar to Figure 4.1:

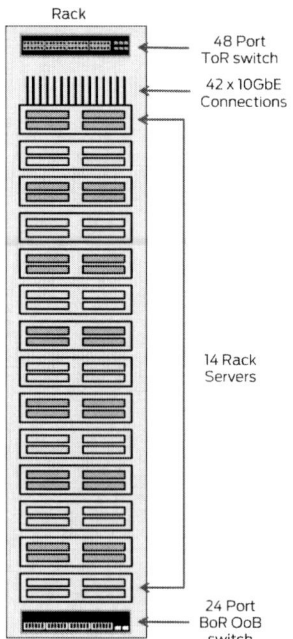

Figure 4.1   **This Book's Rack Design**

Figure 4.1 includes a switch at the bottom of the rack to terminate the OoB 1GbE connections from the servers. Best practice would suggest that the OoB connection on the back of the top-of-rack switch is also connected to this bottom switch, thus providing access to the switch outside of the normal data path while allowing network management traffic and analytics to flow without interruption.

Let's now move on to the spine layer, or aggregation points, per row.

The number of 40GbE connections per a top-of-rack switch is four, and there are ten racks, so our total number of 40GbE connections per a row is 40 x 40GbE. You have the option at this point to either position two spine layer switches, so 20 x 40GbE per spine, or four, which would take that down to 10 x 40GbE per spine. But in order to make this decision you have to work out the subscription ratio of each row.

There are two ways of approaching doing this, either oversubscribe by a factor or two again, or, try and keep the same subscription ratio as prescribed for the leaf to spine.

If you reduce the 400GbE by a factor of two you would have to provision 200GbE of uplink capacity from the spine to the core. If you propose two spines, that would be 100GbE per a spine switch, and if you propose four spines, that would be 50GbE per spine.

With two spines you could propose 3 x 40GbE per spine or with four spines you could propose 2 x 40GbE. In each of these cases you would still be below the initial subscription ratio.

The other option is to propose 100GbE uplinks to the core. With a two-spine solution you could propose 100GbE per spine and with a four-spine design you could propose a 1 x 100GbE per spine, and, in doing so, you would you could keep the same subscription ratio as defined between the leaf and the spine. So the client would see no drop in bandwidth northbound of the top-of-rack switches within each rack.

From a QFX Series point of view, if you go down the 40GbE route then today's choice is the QFX5100-24Q, with its 24 ports of 40GbE plus additional expansion. But if you want the option to do both 40GbE and 100GbE, then the QFX10002, with its flexibility to support both solutions, and its built-in upgrade path from 40GbE to 100GbE, would be the better option. The QFX10002 would also provide additional benefits to the client in regard to its buffer capacity of 300Mb per a port and analytics feature set.

The other option would be the QFX5200 model that also has 40 and 100GbE connectivity, but has a much smaller buffer capacity than the 10K. In each case it provides you with options to present back to the client.

The choice to present either 200GbE or 400GbE uplink capacity from each row to the client, based on their specifications, which would mean a four-rack design per row, would look like Figure 4.2.

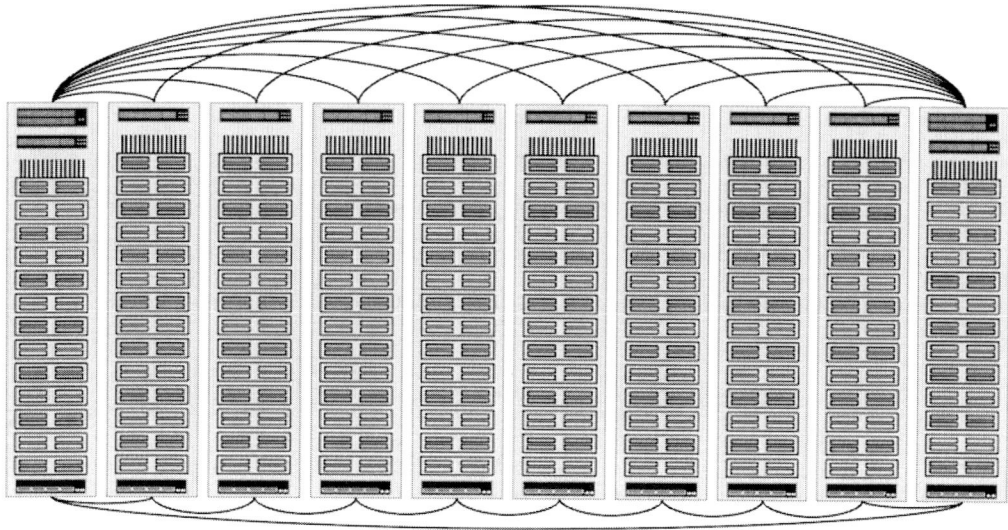

Figure 4.2   DC1 Proposed Data Center Rack Design – Spine and Leaf

And the logical subscription design of Figure 4.2 would look like the one in Figure 4.3, below.

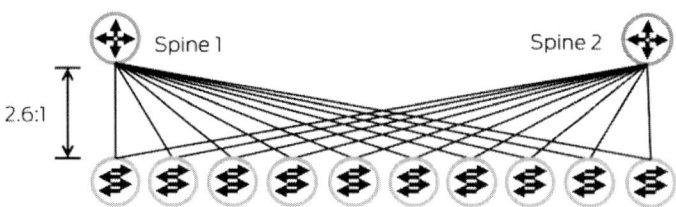

Figure 4.3   Oversubscription Design of DC1 – Spine and Leaf

Now that the number of uplinks from each row is known, you can work out what your core layer product should be. The core layer acts as the point of aggregation between the rows of spine and leaves while providing onward connectivity to the WAN.

As outlined previously, there are five rows of ten racks. Each row of racks will have either 200GbE or 400GbE of uplink connectivity. So, at a minimum, you would have to connect 10 x 100GbE links per core. But, it would also be prudent to make sure you can support the higher capacity, if at some stage the client prefers or wants the higher capacity in the near future.

From the Juniper playbook, the QFX10000 Series precisely fits the bill as it supports 100GbE. The choice is between an eight-slot chassis and a 2RU fixed-format switch. The 2RU platform provides either 12 or 24 ports of 100GbE, while the 13RU chassis can provide up to 240 x 100GbE via a series of line cards. In that case you could have either the 30C line card supporting 30 x 100GbE, or the 36Q, which supports 12 x 100GbE.

The two options are similar in price, but here the 2RU unit is more than sufficient for the proposed client solution. It provides 100% scale even if the client wants a higher capacity bandwidth solution, and it takes up a smaller amount of space, uses less power, and will require less cooling. On that basis it would seem strange to pick a larger chassis when 70% of it would be unused, even if the higher bandwidth solution is chosen.

Utilizing the QFX10002-72Q would mean our rack design would look similar to Figure 4.4.

Chapter 4: Oversubscription

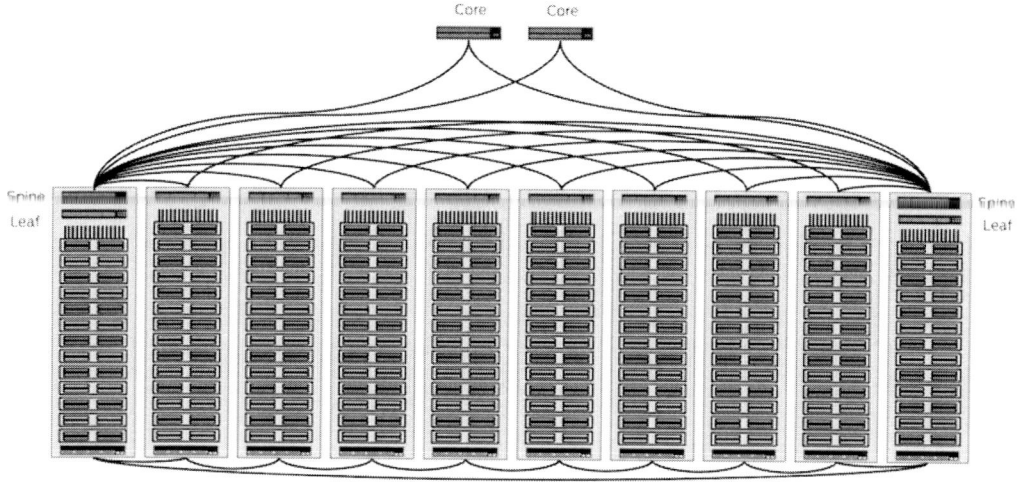

Figure 4.4   DC1 Proposed Data Center Rack Design – Core, Spine, and Leaf

And using the QFX10002-72Q makes the logical subscription design look like Figure 4.5.

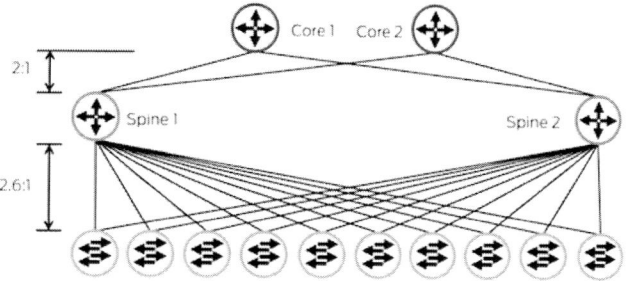

Figure 4.5   Oversubscription Design of DC1 – Core, Spine, and Leaf

The subscription ratio and onward connectivity from the core to the WAN and its MX Series layer, can be treated slightly differently since its generally known that 75% of your traffic stays local to the data center. It seems to be a common traffic profile since servers have moved to a virtual basis and as the applications are more distributed in nature, as are their dependencies. As such, you end up with a 75/25% split in how your traffic traversing your DC, with the 75% local to the Leaf/Spine/Core, and 25% traversing the WAN.

This means you can provision a higher subscription ratio out to the WAN router, which in turn means smaller physical links. Again the choice comes down to 40GbE or 100GbE. While the MX Series supports both, the cost of those interfaces differs a lot as WAN router real estate is quite expensive compared to switching products.

In either case you have the option of 40GbE or 100GbE connectivity from each core switch to the WAN layer. Going 100GbE would be the better option but it may mean additional costs that the client wasn't expecting. If that's the case then it's easy to provision multi-40GbE connections instead. In either case, the logical subscription solution will be similar to that shown in Figure 4.6.

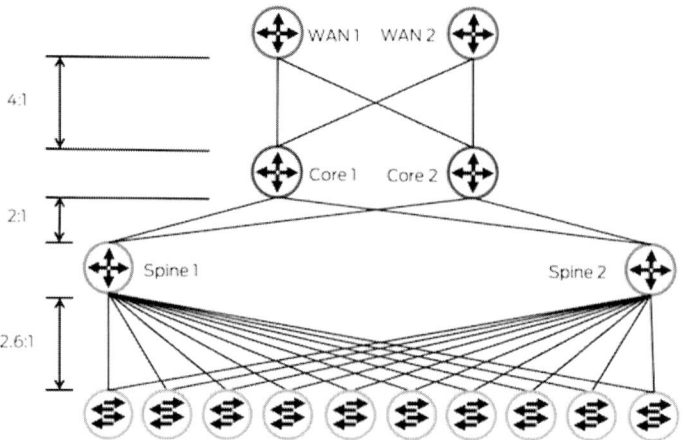

Figure 4.6   Final DC1 Design – WAN, Core, Spine, and Leaf

DC2 Design

The second data center presents a different challenge because the client has stated they would prefer an end-of-row/middle-of-row architecture.

In review of the requirements, DC2 will have five rows of ten racks, the same as DC1, but with each rack housing five blade chassis per rack with each chassis connectivity at four 10GbE. The client would also like a 4:1 or lower subscription ratio, similar to DC1.

So the calculations would be:

- Total per a rack = 4 x 5 (number of 10GbE times number of servers) = 20
- Total per a rack is 20 x 10GbE = 200GbE
- Per a row - 20 x 10 (number of 10GbE per rack times number of racks per row) = 2TB (or 200 x 10GbE per a row)

As opposed to DC1, all of the connections in DC2 have to be connected to the two end-of-row switches. As stated in an earlier chapter, the most efficient way would be to provision two chassis, with one at either end of the rows. Split the connections from each rack by two, so 100 x 10GbE to one end of row and 100 x 10GbE to the other end of row as shown in Figure 4.7, where each cable from each rack is 10 x 10 GbE.

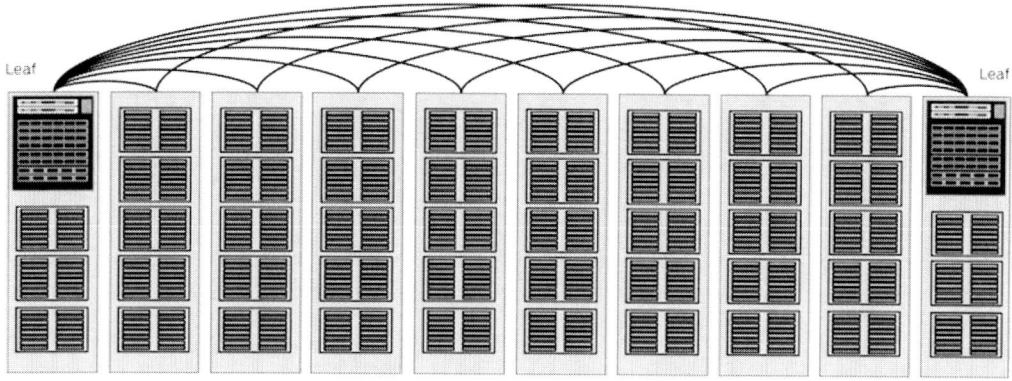

Figure 4.7   DC2's Design – Server to EoR Switch

And from an oversubscription point of view, our first hop from the servers to the end-of-row switches will be at line rate as shown in Figure 4.8 below.

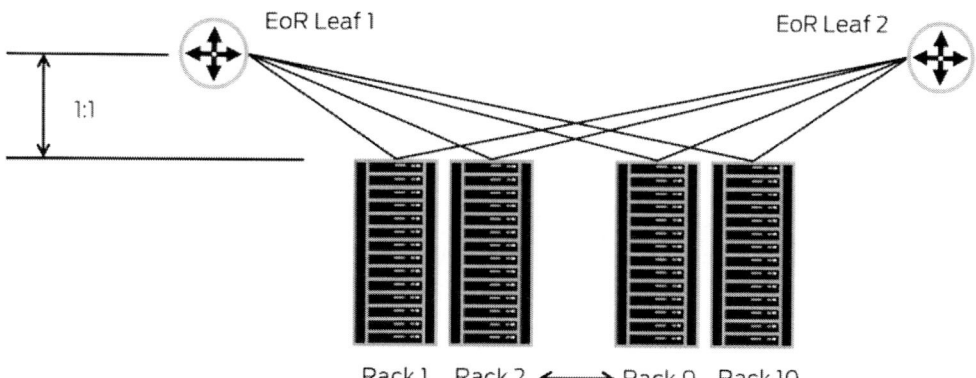

Figure 4.8   DC2's Oversubscription - Server to EoR

With this in mind the first point of concern for oversubscription is from the leaf layer to the spine layer. With 100 x 10GbE per leaf, or 1TB, and an oversubscription ratio of at least 4:1 would mean 1TB divided by 4 equals 250GbE of uplink connectivity to the spine layer.

The ideal product for the leaf layer would be the QFX10008 chassis. It has eight slots, so plenty of room for expansion if additional blade servers are installed into the racks, and it also has a range of line cards to suit any combination of connectivity. The main line card of interest is the 60S-6Q, which has 60 ports of 10GbE plus six extra uplink ports supporting either 6 x 40GbE, or 2 x 100GbE. You could take the 100 x 10GbE rack connections, divide these over two 60S line cards, and then use the two 100GbE uplink ports from each line card to connect to the spine layer. This would drop the oversubscription ratio by half, as the ratio would be based on 50 x 10GbE ports per line card and 2 x 100GbE uplinks. So, 500 divided by 200 (total bandwidth of incoming connections / total bandwidth of uplinks) = 2.5 to 1, well within the clients oversubscription ratio.

So our logical oversubscription design would look like the one illustrated in Figure 4.9.

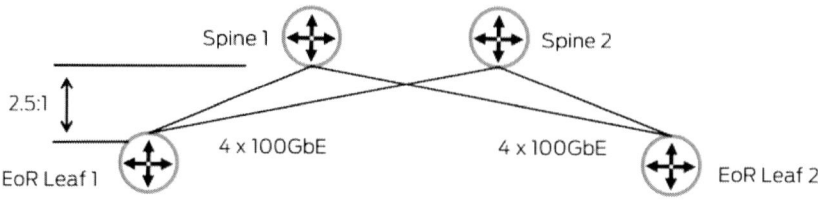

Figure 4.9   DC2 Oversubscription Ratio

The effect of provisioning 4 x 100GbE per leaf is that the spine layer has to accommodate 8 x 100GbE per row and with ten rows that's 80 x 100GbE across two spine switches. Given the quantity of 100GbE that's required, the choice of spine layer device is made for us in the guise of the QFX10008 chassis.

The most suitable line cards are either the 36Q, which supports 12 ports of 100GbE, or the 30C, which 30 ports of 100GbE Both line cards also provide breakout options for 40GbE and 10GbE, so you don't have to provision additional line cards for those connectivity options. If you remove cost concerns from this design, then the 30C line card is the obvious choice because you can have two line cards per spine, providing 60 x 100GbE ports. But when you factor cost concerns into this design, then it might be slightly more economical to place four 36Q line cards per spine than two 30Cs.

So the physical diagram for DC2 would look like Figure 4.10.

Chapter 4: Oversubscription 43

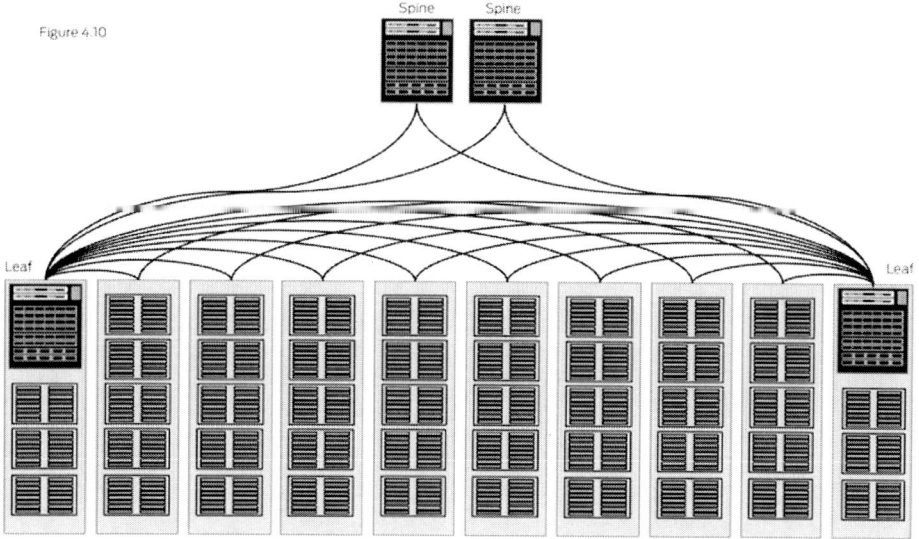

Figure 4.10 **DC2 Spine and Leaf Design**

NOTE   Notice that both Figure 4.9 and Figure 4.11 consolidate the number of layers by using an end-of-row design. The leaf nodes are now in the end-of-row position and the spine layer now moves up to become what was the core layer. So the principle of spine and leaf stays the same regardless of whether you use top-of-rack or end-of-row design.

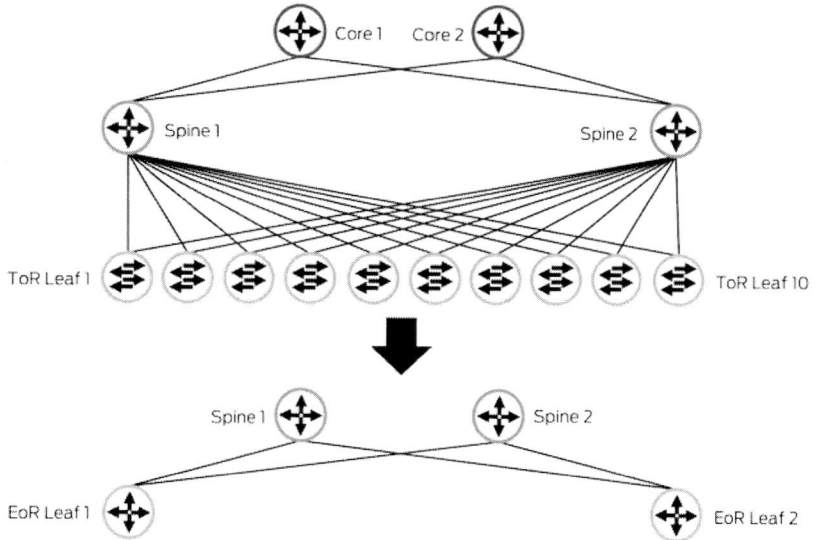

Figure 4.11 **DC2 – The Difference Between DC1 and DC2 Spine and Leaf**

If you follow the same principle for connectivity to the WAN layer as designed for DC1, whereby 75% of the traffic would be local to the spine and leaf and 25% over the WAN, then the connectivity would consist of either several 40GbE interfaces from both spines to the WAN layer, or you could provision 100GbE, but again, that's an option to offer to the client.

In each case, the logical oversubscription solution will look like the one shown in Figure 4.12.

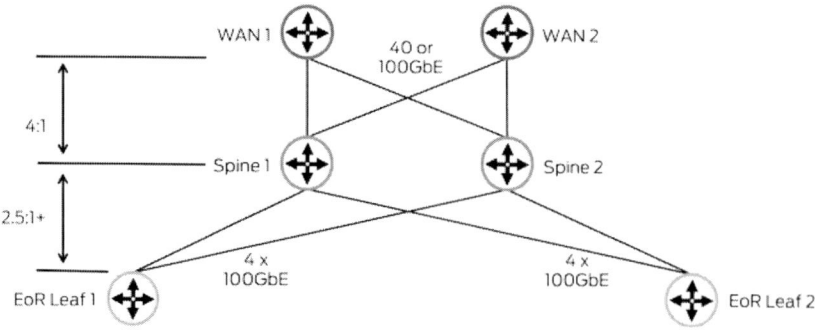

Figure 4.12   DC2 to WAN Oversubscription

So now that the designs for DC1 and DC2 are established, let's move on to logical design and consider the different options available using the same client requirements as stated at the beginning of this chapter.

Additional Points to Consider

One element not touched upon is support for 1GbE-based servers. In the scenario for DC1 any one of the servers in the rack design can be multi-1GbE, but what changes is that the total connection bandwidth to the top-of-rack switch would be reduced, and as such the uplink bandwidth from that top-of-rack/leaf to the spine in that row may be slightly lower. If you run through the calculations again you'll find you may only need a 10GbE uplink connectivity as opposed to 40GbE. In each case, bear in mind the requirements and the subscription ratio you need to attain.

From a physical point of view the type of switch you could use to support 1GbE might also change. The QFX5100 series supports 1GbE copper natively via a 1GbE copper SFP. If the number of 1GbE connections is greater than the number of 10GbE server connections, and you suspect that there will be no migration to 10GbE servers, then consider the EX4300 switch as an option. If, on the other hand, there is likely to be a migration to 10GbE in the near future, keep the QFX5100 and use optics to connect the 1GbE requirement. It will save a full switch swap-out in the future.

Chapter 5

Fabric Architecture

In this chapter we move from the physical applications of data center design discussed in Chapter 4 to the different logical architectures that Juniper provides. When discussing logical design, this *Day One* book refers to the IP addressing structure and the Layer 2 and Layer 3 transport mechanisms — essentially the control plane and data plane of the design. Juniper provides you with several options, from single switch management with multiple transport mechanisms, to virtualizing the control plane across multiple switches creating a fabric with a single point of management.

First of all, why do we need a logical network? This question arises every time there is an increased need to scale the network in order to support new technologies such as virtualization.

There are protocol and control mechanisms that limit the disastrous effects of a topology loops in the network. Spanning Tree Protocol (STP) has been the primary solution to this problem because it provides a loop-free Layer 2 environment. Even though STP has gone through a number of enhancements and extensions, and even though it scales to very large network environments, it still only provides a single active path from one device to another, regardless of how many actual connections might exist in the network. So although STP is a robust and scalable solution to redundancy in a Layer 2 network, the single logical link creates two problems: at least half of the available system bandwidth is off-limits to data traffic, and when network topology changes occur they can take longer to resolve than most applications will accept without loss of traffic. Rapid Spanning Tree Protocol (RSTP) reduces the overhead of the rediscovery process, and it allows a Layer 2 network to reconverge faster, but the delay is still high.

Link aggregation (IEEE 802.3ad) solves some of these problems by enabling the use of more than one link connection between switches. All physical connections are considered one logical connection. The problem with standard link aggregation is that the connections are point-to-point.

So in order to remove STP and its somewhat limited functionality, Juniper, like other vendors, came up with a series of different logical solutions for the network that eliminate the reconvergence issue and utilize 100% of all available bandwidth.

Juniper's architectures are based on the principle of a common physical platform centered on the QFX Series, but supporting different logical solutions. This approach provides you with the flexibility to support different options and fit the scenario you need, but it also means that if your requirements change you can adapt both the physical and logical structure without costly repurchases.

Juniper offers five logical architectures: two of them are open standards (1 and 5), and three are Juniper-based solutions (2, 3, and 4):

1. Traditional – MC-LAG (multichassis link aggregation group)

2. Virtual Chassis

3. Virtual Chassis Fabric

4. Junos Fusion

5. IP clos fabrics

Let's use the requirements for DC1 and DC2 architectures outlined in Chapter 4 as the basis of a fabric architecture discussion, so each logical offering can be imposed over the top of the physical architecture. Along the way this chapter outlines the details of each solution, its merits, and which may be more appropriate to which design. Let's use the solutions created in Chapter 4, minus the WAN layer, and use Figure 5.1 for this chapter's base physical architecture.

Chapter 5: Fabric Architecture

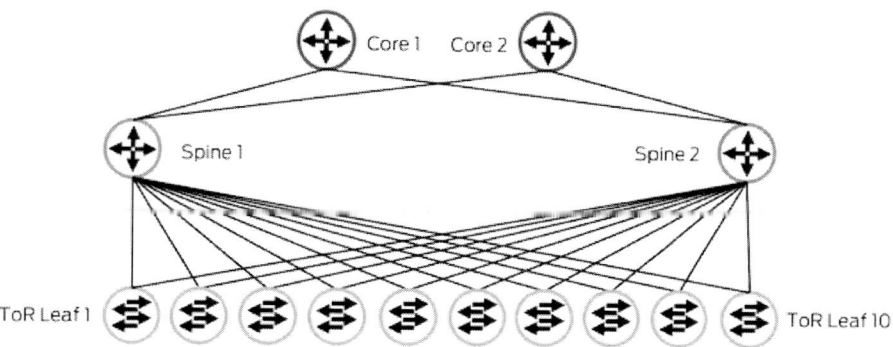

Figure 5.1   Chapter 5 Base Physical Architecture

Traditional – MC-LAG

Our starting point is MC-LAG, which enable a client device to form a logical link aggregation group (LAG) interface between two MC-LAG peers. An MC-LAG provides redundancy and load balancing between the two MC-LAG peers, multi-homing support, and a loop-free Layer 2 network without running STP.

In Figure 5.2, on one end of an MC-LAG is an MC-LAG client device, such as a server or switch, which has one or more physical links in a LAG. This client device uses the link as a LAG and traffic is distributed across all links in the LAG. On the other side of the MC-LAG, there are two MC-LAG peers. Each of the MC-LAG peers has one or more physical links connected to a single client device.

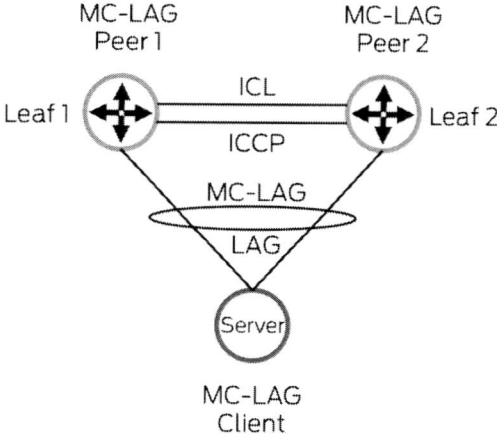

Figure 5.2   Basic MC-LAG

The MC-LAG peers use Inter-Chassis Control Protocol (ICCP) to exchange control information and coordinate with each other to ensure that data traffic is forwarded properly. ICCP replicates control traffic and forwarding states across the MC-LAG peers and communicates the operational state of the MC-LAG members. Because ICCP uses Transmission Control Protocol/ Internet Protocol (TCP/IP) to communicate between the peers, the two peers must be connected to each other. ICCP messages exchange MC-LAG configuration parameters and ensure that both peers use the correct Link Aggregation Control Protocol (LACP) parameters.

The interchassis control link (ICL), also known as the interchassis control link-protection link (ICL-PL), is used to forward data traffic across the MC-LAG peers. This link provides redundancy when a link failure (for example, an MC-LAG trunk failure) occurs on one of the active links. The ICL can be a single physical Ethernet interface or an aggregated Ethernet interface. You can configure only one ICL between the two MC-LAG peers, although you can configure multiple MC-LAGs between them.

LACP is a subcomponent of the IEEE 802.3ad standard and is used to discover multiple links from a client device connected to an MC-LAG peer. LACP must be configured on both MC-LAG peers for an MC-LAG to work correctly.

Figures 5.3 and 5.4 show that MC-LAG can be configured in active/standby mode, where only one device actively forwards traffic, or in active/active mode, in which both devices actively forward traffic. In active/standby mode, only one of the MC-LAG peers is active at any given time. The other MC-LAG peer is in backup (standby) mode. The active MC-LAG peer uses the LACP to advertise to client devices that its child link is available for forwarding data traffic.

In active/active mode, Figure 5.4, you can see that all member links are active on the MC-LAG, as opposed to Figure 5.3, which shows active/standby mode. In active/active mode, media access control (MAC) addresses learned on one MC-LAG peer are propagated to the other MC-LAG peer.

In most cases active/active is the preferred mode.

- Traffic is load-balanced in active/active mode, resulting in 100% use of all links.

Chapter 5: Fabric Architecture   49

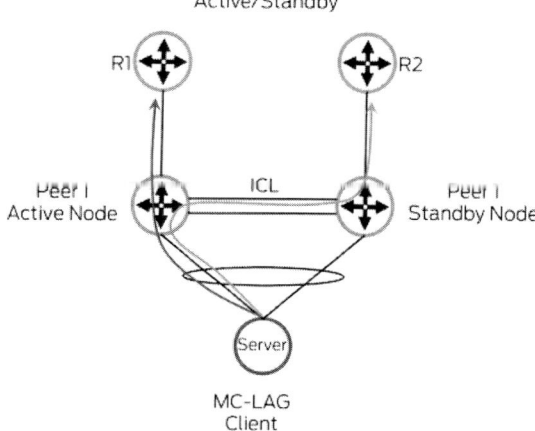

Figure 5.3   **MC-LAG Active / Standby Mode**

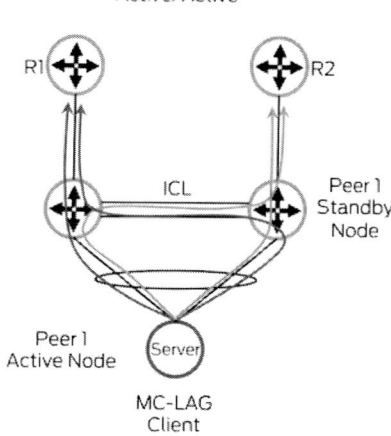

Figure 5.4   **MC-LAG Active / Active Mode**

- Convergence is faster in active/active mode than in active/standby mode. In active/active mode, information is exchanged between devices during operations. After a failure, the operational switch or router does not need to relearn any routes and continues to forward traffic.

- Active/active mode enables you to configure Layer 3 protocols on integrated routing and bridging (IRB) interfaces, providing a hybrid Layer 2 and Layer 3 environment.

But how does this relate to the DC1 and DC2 scenarios? The quick answer is: *it depends*. Recall that in earlier chapters, our two options were spine and leaf in the form of a top-of-rack and a spine and leaf in an end-of-row topology.

MC-LAG relates to Layer 2-based solutions and as such if your proposed network is going to have Layer 2 VLANs present at both the leaf layer and the spine layer, in both solutions, then you are going to need MC-LAG at either the spine layer for DC1 and either the spine or leaf layer for DC2. As Figure 5.5 shows, the spine layer would have to be interconnected to each other for a MC-LAG to work. It also means your MC-LAG setup for every Layer 2 domain is present at a central point in the network, as opposed to distributed between multiple leaf devices, which is possible but can be messy.

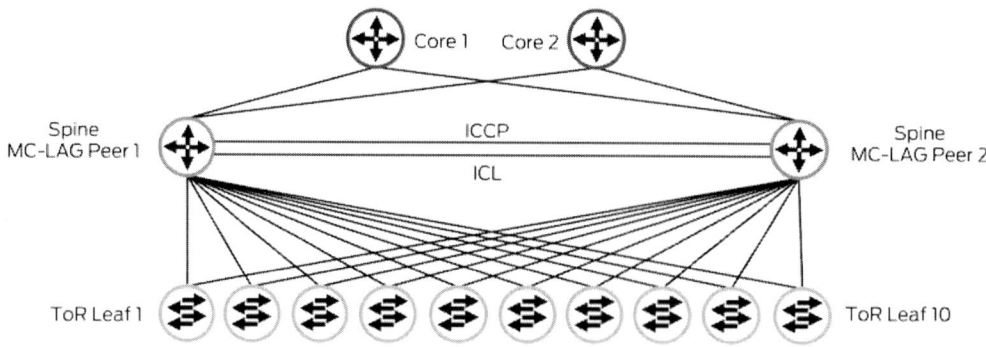

Figure 5.5   MC-LAG Architecture for DC1

With the DC2 logical architecture you have the option to implement one step closer to the server layer at the leaf layer as shown in Figure 5.6.

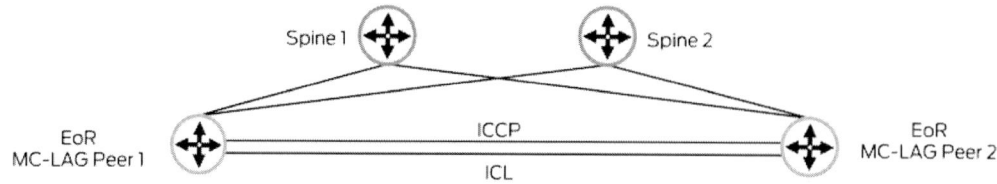

Figure 5.6   MC-LAG Architecture for DC2

Now the question is, should you implement MC-LAG in either of these scenarios? I would suggest not. Solutions like VCF, Junos Fusion, and a Layer 3 IP Clos with a Layer 2 overlay would be far better solutions, and they scale considerably further and with less management overhead. Where MC-LAG setups do become relevant is when you don't want a proprietary fabric or an IP fabric but need a failover architecture for a small deployment of QFX Series in a data center. In this instance, MC-LAG would be appropriate and is fully supported across all QFX Series platforms.

MORE? For more detailed information on MC-LAG and the QFX Series refer to the following link, which outlines configuration examples and best practices: http://www.juniper.net/techpubs/en_US/junos/information-products/pathway-pages/mc-lag/multichassis-link-aggregation-groups.html.

Virtual Chassis

Juniper released Virtual Chassis on the EX4200 Series Ethernet Switch in 2009 as an alternative to the stacking technologies that were, and are still, present. The basic principle in Virtual Chassis is to take the benefits of a single control plane in a chassis and virtualize it over a series of distributed switches interconnected via a cable backplane. It allows the management of up to ten switches to be simplified via a single management interface, so you have a common Junos OS version across all switches, a single configuration file, and an intuitive chassis-like slot and module/port interface numbering scheme.

The design is further simplified through a single control plane and the ability to aggregate interfaces across Virtual Chassis switch members as you would with a normal chassis.

Switches within a Virtual Chassis are assigned one of three roles; *master RE (Router Engine)*, *backup RE*, and *line card*. As the name implies, the master RE is the main routing engine for the Virtual Chassis. It acts as the main point of configuration and holds the main routing table, which is copied to each Virtual Chassis member to provide local, or distributed, switching and routing.

The backup provides a backup to the master RE and it is ready to take over mastership of the Virtual Chassis in the event of a failure of the master. The backup maintains a copy of the switching and routing tables and when an update to the master is enacted, then the backup RE automatically updates its tables. Think of it as an active/active sync.

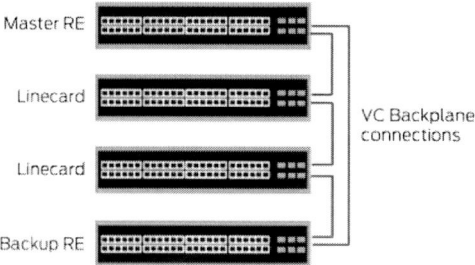

Figure 5.7   Virtual Chassis Switch Roles

All other switches are classed as line cards and in the event a master RE goes down and the backup RE takes over mastership, then a switch member classed as a line card automatically becomes the backup RE. In reality, when the old master RE has resolved its issue, it should come back as either the master or new backup. You have the flexibility to select the best option depending on your needs.

The special sauce that makes all this possible is Juniper's proprietary protocol called, unsurprisingly, Virtual Chassis Control Protocol (VCCP). It's based on Intermediate System-to-Intermediate System (IS-IS), which is a link state protocol. It's based on the principle of discovering, maintaining, and then flooding topology information on the shortest paths across the Virtual Chassis to all members with the most efficient routes on a flow-by-flow basis. VCCP is not user-configurable, and operates automatically, on both the rear-panel and front-facing Virtual Chassis ports.

So how does Virtual Chassis apply to this book's data center solution? Besides the EX Series lineage and tradition, Virtual Chassis is also supported on the QFX5100 Series and that gives you the option to contrast a Virtual Chassis for both the top-of-rack and end-of-row data centers.

In fact, the ability to mix and match different switch types in a single Virtual Chassis is a fundamental feature and Virtual Chassis supports these different Juniper Networks EX Series switching platforms:

- EX4200
- EX4550
- EX4300
- EX4600
- QFX5100

The EX4200 and EX4550 can be part of the same Virtual Chassis, and the EX4300 and EX4600 can be part of the same Virtual Chassis, but you can also mix the EX4300 and the QFX5100 in the same Virtual Chassis, which could be an option in our DC1 and DC2 to support 100/1000Mbps interfaces as well as 10GbE in the same virtual switch. Let's investigate the design option as shown in Figure 5.8.

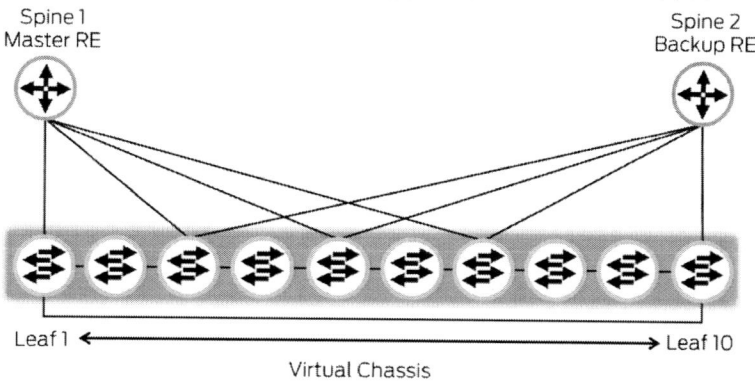

Figure 5.8   Virtual Chassis Architecture for DC1

For DC1, Virtual Chasis could run the entire top-of-rack switches on a rack-by-rack basis. This would give a common fabric at the rack layer, while allowing traffic to switch locally without having to traverse the spine layer, as all members of the Virtual Chassis to be interconnected (hence the Virtual Chasis flow in Figure 5.8). The oversubscription ratio would stay the same and even be reduced slightly due to the local switching at the rack layer.

But the cabling costs go up and you have to provision additional cables between each of the switches. Also, traffic isn't using the most efficient route to get to its destination, as traffic from top-of-rack 1 would need to pass through all of the other switches to get to top-of-rack10. This is due to Virtual Chassis assigning a higher weighting in its calculation than sending the traffic externally up to the spine and down to top-of-rack 10, even though that's the more efficient route. The other negative factor is scale. While the requirements are for ten switches over ten racks, what if you need to introduce more switches, or create a secondary Virtual Chassis in the same racks? Either situation would just add to the complexity of the solution.

This is why Virtual Chassis Fabric was introduced, to allow you to take the best elements of Virtual Chassis and institute better scale and traffic distribution. It's discussed in the next section.

For DC2, Virtual Chassis only works well when you introduce a stack-based solution into the two end-of-row cabinets as opposed to a chassis, as shown in Figure 5.9. The limitations still exist, however, which means that while a small implementation of Virtual Chassis could work, you are still going to be limited by the backplane capacity. In a Virtual Chassis this is comprised of a number of Virtual Chassis port (VCP) links and could lead to a higher internal oversubscription because your traffic distribution won't take the most efficient path, because traffic potentially still needs to pass through multiple switches to reach a destination.

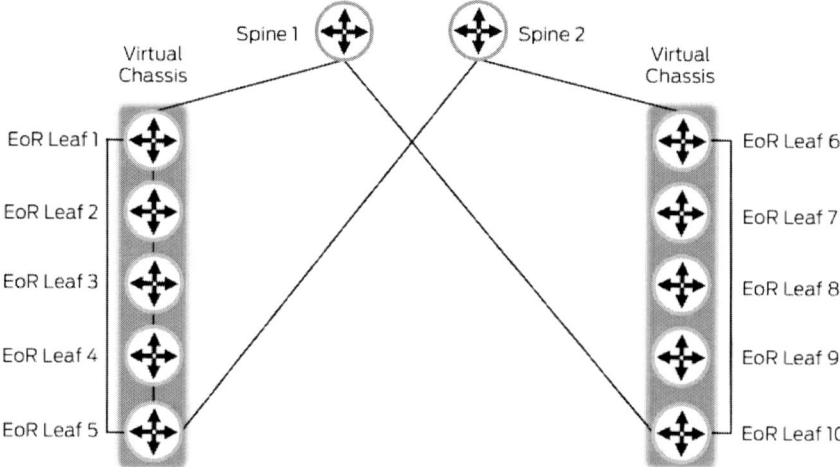

Figure 5.9   Virtual Chassis Architecture for DC2

So while Virtual Chassis is an option, I would suggest that Virtual Chassis favors small data center deployment solutions as opposed to anything at scale. Remember, it's a great campus technology and it does offer some excellent options, but there are other DC fabric designs that provide more robust solutions, as is outlined in the next section.

Virtual Chassis Fabric

Virtual Chassis Fabric takes the principles of Virtual Chassis with a single control plane over multiple switches, but goes much larger in scale, supports multiple higher port types (1/10/40GbE), and introduces the IP Clos topology that simplifies the fabric.

What is a fabric? A data center fabric is a system of switches and servers and all the interconnections between them that visually resemble a fabric. A data center fabric allows for a simple flattened architecture where any connecting device is only a single hop away.

The flattened architecture of fabrics is key to their agility. Fabrics are comprised of two elements, a leaf and a spine, which are configured in a hub and spoke design. The leaf node provides the connectivity to servers while the spine provides the aggregation point for various leaves as shown in Figure 5.10.

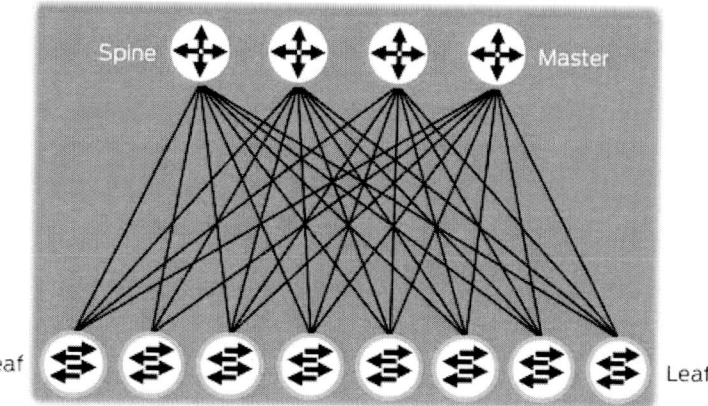

Figure 5.10   Virtual Chassis Fabric Leaf and Spine

Virtual Chassis versus Virtual Chassis Fabric Comparisons

In a spine and leaf topology, the total number of distinct paths between two leaf devices is equal to the number of spine devices. In Figure 5.11, each leaf device has four connections to four spine switches, and as such, it has four paths to every other leaf switch. If any link goes down, it will end up having fewer paths. But as long as there is more than one such path, traffic will be distributed on all available paths.

As a result, it provides a distinct advantage over Virtual Chassis in that every location within the fabric is only two hops away, as opposed to Virtual Chassis where a destination could be up to nine hops away.

With Virtual Chassis Fabric's increase in scale you can now move past the limitations of Virtual Chassis, which only allows up to 10 members to be virtualized in to a single solution. Virtual Chassis Fabric allows up to 20 switches, with either two or four spines and 16 or 18 leaves, allowing you to build a single virtual switch to support up to 864 x 10GbE ports per Virtual Chassis Fabric if you use 48 port leaf switches and 1,728 x 10GbE if you were to use 96 port leaf switches.

The principle of a master and backup in an active/passive routing engine stays the same as outlined in Virtual Chassis but generally we now elect the spine layer switches as the *master* and *backup* utilizing a single virtual MAC and IP gateway. All other switches in the Virtual Chassis Fabric become line cards of the master. There's a single point of CLI through the master, and there's a distributed forwarding plane so every switch has a copy of the both the Layer 2 and 3 tables.

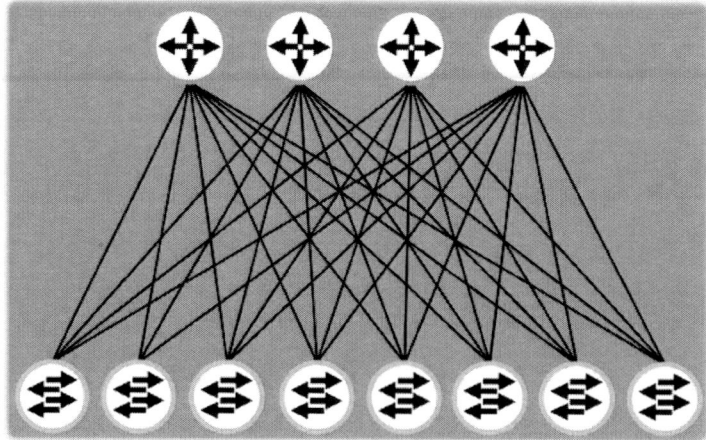

Figure 5.11   Master, Backup, and Line Card Placement

With Virtual Chassis Fabric you also gain the option of plug and play implementation. In the existing Virtual Chassis, you had to designate the master and backup, and then you could pre-prevision the other members of the Virtual Chassis though configuring the serial numbers into the master so the master knew what line cards would be members. That option still exists, but you also have the option to pre-prevision just the master and backup at the spine layer and any other nodes that are directly connected to any of the spine nodes are allowed to join the Virtual Chassis automatically without pre-provisioning their serial numbers. In this mode, leaf nodes can be brought into the Virtual Chassis Fabric without any user intervention – their configuration, VCP port conversions and dynamic software update will be handled automatically through the use of the open standard LLDP (Link Layer Discovery Protocol).

With the higher bandwidth achieved through Virtual Chassis Fabric, the way traffic paths are calculated has changed as well. In a Virtual Chassis system the shortest path calculation strictly followed the Dijkstra algorithm, which evaluated both the number of hops and link bandwidth between members of the Virtual Chassis. But, even when there were multiple equal cost paths between two devices, only one path would be used for data traffic.

In Virtual Chassis Fabric, the VCCP protocol is enhanced to discover all distinct paths. When multiple paths are discovered, traffic is now load-balanced across these multiple paths and these paths are formed into virtual trunks or aggregated links. Virtual Chassis Fabric has two types of trunks: *next hop trunks* (NH trunks) and *remote destination trunks* (RD trunks). NH trunks are trunks that are for devices that are directly connected to each other, such as between a leaf and a spine, and when there are multiple links between two physical devices, a VCP trunk is created to simplify topology.

To achieve load balancing across multiple paths, VCCP was enhanced further to create a trunk to each remote destination node. So if traffic from one leaf needs to get to another leaf via the spine layer, the VCCP algorithm also takes into account the paths to the remote destination when calculating the best path and forming a virtual trunk to that destination.

To remove the possibly of congestion, the VCCP protocol also takes into account the bandwidth of each link, and implements a fair weight algorithm so each node or switch in the Virtual Chassis Fabric can spray traffic across the fabric on a flow-by-flow basis – VCCP considers the bandwidth on each link, both physically and to its remote destination, and automatically adjusting traffic on a link-by-link basis to avoid congestion and deliver packets in order. The protocol that does this is *Adaptive Flowlet Splicing*.

Virtual Chassis Fabric in DC1 and DC2

So how does Virtual Chassis Fabric help us in our two DC scenarios? For DC1, which follows a top-of-rack topology, Virtual Chassis Fabric is a perfect fit. Our top-of-rack switches become leafs with connectivity up to the spine layer. Our two spine switches become master RE and backup RE and all of our leaves become line cards as shown in Figure 5.12.

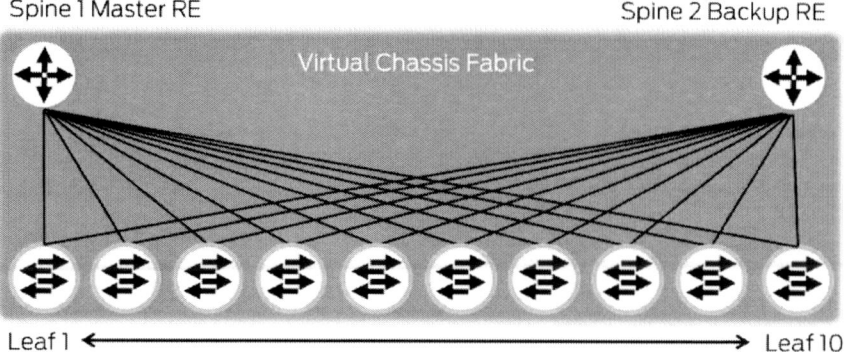

Figure 5.12   Virtual Chassis Fabric in DC1

As you can see in Figure 5.12, the links between leaf and spine now become Virtual Chassis Ports and allow the Virtual Chassis Fabric to become a single fabric over which traffic will be distributed. Northbound connectivity from the Virtual Chassis Fabric to the core is via the spine layer advertised with the single IP gateway for the Virtual Chassis Fabric. The purpose of the core layer in this design is to provide a point of aggregation for the Virtual Chassis Fabric to connect to the other Virtual Chassis Fabrics present in the other rows. You can also LAG the links up to the core to allow traffic to be distributed to both spines as shown in Figure 5.13.

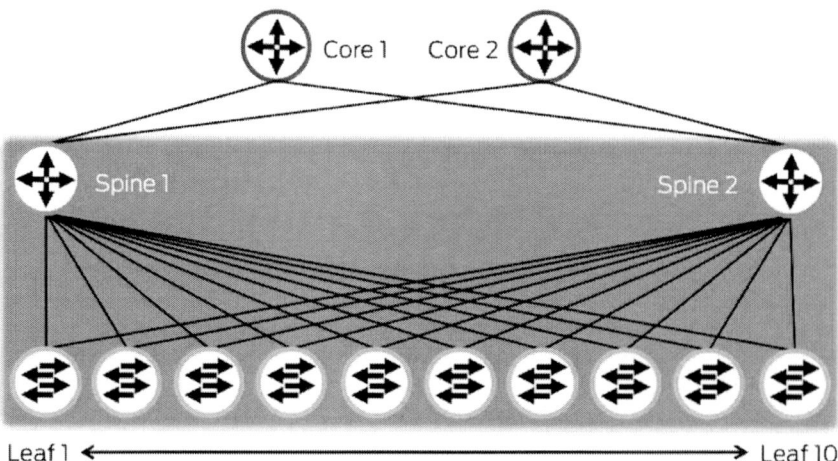

Figure 5.13   Virtual Chassis Fabric in DC1 with Core Layer

This design can then be replicated over the other rows of racks allowing what were 50 racks of switches to be virtualized into five IP addresses and five points of management for the whole of DC1.

Virtual Chassis Fabric also provides full support for SDN-controller based solutions integrated with virtual servers which is covered in Chapter 9.

For DC2, which uses an end-of-row based solution, Virtual Chassis Fabric becomes a little more challenging. With all of the switches located in single racks at each end of the row you would need to implement a spine in each row and then interconnect each leaf across the rows to reach each spine (as shown in Figure 5.14) to allow the Virtual Chassis Fabric to form. As noted earlier, for a Virtual Chassis Fabric to form every leaf needs to be directly connected to each spine layer. This would increase cabling issues and costs. The other option would be to implement a Virtual Chassis Fabric-per-end-of-row, with two spines and rest of the switches as leafs, but stacked. That would provide a single point of management the same as a chassis would provide, but would require a major increase in cabling as you would have to follow the same principles of leaf and spine connectivity but within a single rack. In addition, the oversubscription ratio is different for DC2 and as such would need to increase the cabling at 40GbE to make a Virtual Chassis Fabric work.

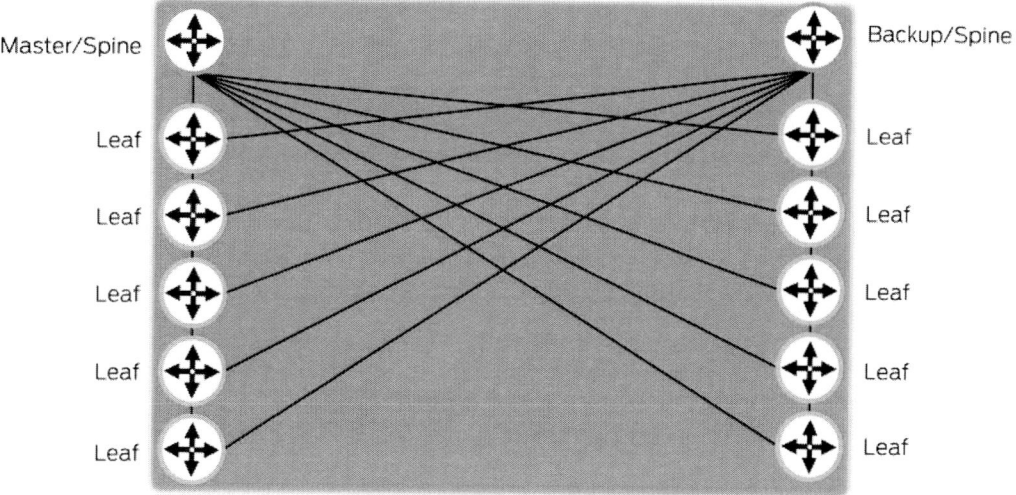

Figure 5.14   DC2 Virtual Chassis Fabric Stretch Over a Row of Racks

This is why you need to work through the pros and cons for each scenario. Virtual Chassis Fabric works really well for a top-of-rack based solution, but for end-of-row it becomes a little more problematic and I suspect it would still be better to position a chassis for the end-of-row solution as opposed to individual switches.

Our next architecture takes many of the principles of Virtual Chassis and Virtual Chassis Fabric and enlarges the scale of the number of switches you can virtualize.

Junos Fusion

Junos Fusion is a new technology from Juniper, which, at its most basic, takes the elements of Virtual Chassis Fabric, such as the single management domain, the removal of spanning tree, and the full bandwidth use, and expands the support up to 128 switches per virtualized domain while simplifying the management of all those switches through the use of a new software implementation.

The Junos Fusion architecture is comprised of *Aggregation Devices* (QFX10000 switches) and *Satellite Devices* (EX43000 and/or QFX5000 switches). Satellite devices directly connect to the aggregation device in a hub and spoke topology as shown in Figure 5.15.

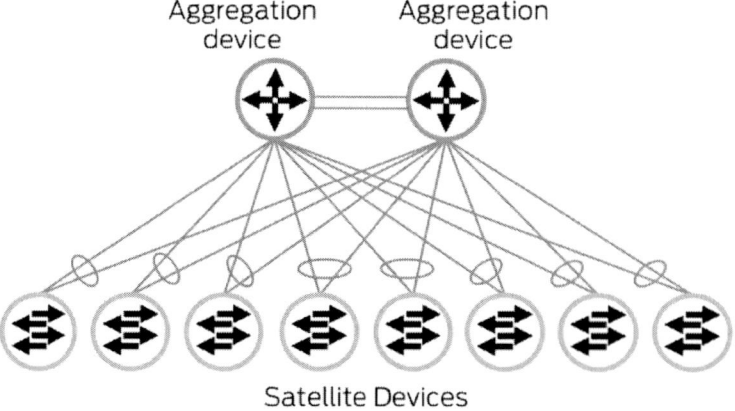

Figure 5.15   Junos Fusion Setup

The key characteristic of Junos Fusion is that satellite devices can be managed either by a single aggregation device or a pair of aggregation devices. Think of the satellite devices as line cards of the aggregation device but with the feature set of the aggregation devices. This provides customers with simplicity of operations, enabling them to manage a large data center from just a pair of switches (aggregation devices) without having to actively manage any of the top-of-rack switches, since they are managed centrally from the aggregation devices.

How Junos Fusion Compares to Virtual Chassis Fabric?

The key difference between Junos Fusion and Virtual Chassis Fabric is that Virtual Chassis Fabric is comprised entirely of switches that use Broadcom PFEs. As a result, they use a fabric protocol called HiGig to communicate within the Virtual Chassis Fabric architecture. In Junos Fusion, since the architecture consists of combining systems with both Broadcom PFEs and Juniper's own Q5 ASIC (on the QFX10000), the HiGig protocol isn't used. Instead, Junos Fusion uses the open standard IEEE 802.1BR bridge port extension protocol to communicate between various devices, an open, standards-based mechanism to remotely manage top-of-rack switches or satellites devices.

Another key difference is scale. While Virtual Chassis Fabric scales to about 20 racks, Junos Fusion scales to a much higher 128 racks, or 128 satellites.

Some of the key attributes of aggregation devices within the Junos Fusion architecture are:

- One or more switches that manage satellite devices (top-of-rack switches) remotely
- Configuration, software image management, statistics polling from satellite devices
- The system supports an option to replicate the configuration between aggregation devices. Satellite devices do not need to keep a local configuration copies.
- Automated discovery and provisioning of satellite devices
- In-band connectivity for management of satellite devices
- Junos OS support with central upgrade process of the satellite devices. Junos Fusion has been designed in such a way that all components are loosely coupled. This allows us to introduce the notion of "software upgrade groups." Devices within the same SUG, or software upgrade group, need to run the same OS. A given Junos Fusion system can have as many SUGs as the opera-

tor prefers, and the OS across different SUGs does not have to be the same. This enables operational simplicity and ease of maintenance.

- Supported Aggregation Device: QFX10002-72Q, 36Q, QFX10008, and QFX10016

- Cascade ports (satellite ports) can be used as regular L2 or L3 ports for connecting any type of devices such as firewalls and load-balancers

And some of the key attributes of satellite devices within the Junos Fusion architecture are:

- Standard top-of-rack switches managed remotely by one or more aggregation devices

- No local management required

- Can be single or dual-homed to aggregation devices

- Satellite devices run Windriver Yocto Linux or Linux Forwarding Engine OS (LFE OS) using considerably less space than a normal Junos software image, thus making the upgrade process faster

- Supported Satellite Device: EX4300 and QFX5100 switches

One attribute not highlighted above is licensing. Because the Junos Fusion satellite devices essentially inherent the features of the aggregation device, the protocols supported on the aggregation device are now present on the satellite, which means you now only place the license at the aggregation. So if you need OSPF at the server layer, then once the satellite is plugged in and registered, it will have full OSPF but without the need for the additional license.

Junos Fusion in DC1 and DC2

So how does Junos Fusion help with the two DC scenarios in this chapter? For DC 1 it can change the architecture of the design as we now can remove the spine layer and allow the top-of-rack switches to connect directly to the core layer, due to the fact that Junos Fusion doesn't support a tiered layer approach. This would allow you to reduce the number of devices in the solution by removing a layer of the network and you simplify the management domain as all switches in all rows are now under the same single point of management.

Note that there are changes whose effects can be significant for the client. The first change is that the new spine/core layer will need to increase to accommodate the number of 40GbE connections that are now coming firstly from each top-of-rack switch. This has the effect of increasing the cost of the solution as core devices are swapped for larger chassis-based switches and you increase the number of 40GbE line cards. While increasing the cost of the core/spine there is also the increase in cost of fiber connectivity as each top-of-rack now connects to a central core switch.

NOTE Junos Fusion comes with a lot of failure protections built-in, and, for the sake of brevity, they are not covered here, but Junos Fusion is a active/active control plane across the data center, and as such the potential for a control plane failure affecting the whole data center should be a concern you need to understand so you can incorporate its management into your best practices.

Is Junos Fusion an option for DC1? Yes, if you want to simplify the management domain to cover a large number of switches while providing an easy point of configuration and management.

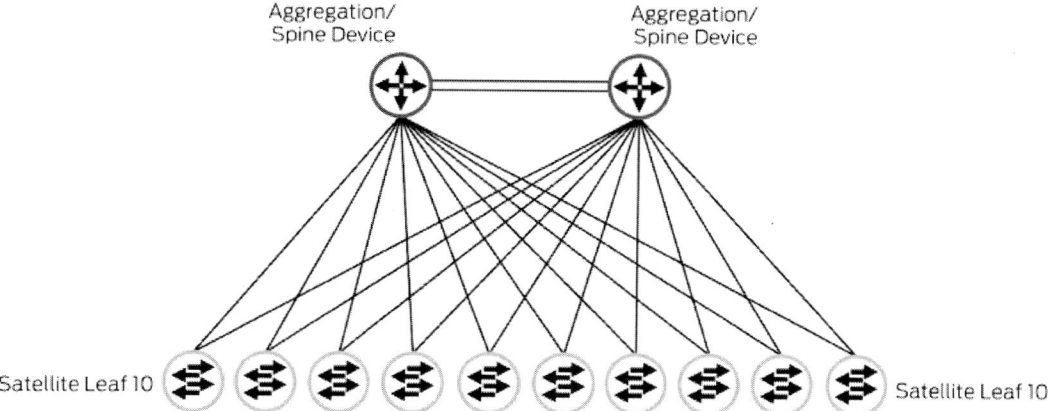

Figure 5.16 Junos Fusion in VC1

As for DC2, the potential issue with Junos Fusion is the same as implementing Virtual Chassis Fabric. You're dependent on 1RU QFX devices to do the 10GbE termination in both solutions. This would mean implementing stacks of 1RU switches and connecting those satellite devices back to the core/aggregation layer. The benefit of the chassis solution is that local switching is done via the backplane on the chassis, as opposed to pushing the traffic up to the core and potentially back down to the leaf layer.

Again, this is why Juniper provides you with options, because one solution does not always fit all scenarios, and while Junos Fusion works well for DC1 more than DC2, maybe an IP fabric as outlined in Chapter 6 could provide a solution for both.

MORE? For more detailed information about Junos Fusion and data centers, see the Juniper/O'Reilly book, *The QFX10000 Series*, by Douglas Hanks (O'Reilly Media, 2016), at http://www.juniper.net/books.

Chapter 6

IP Fabrics and BGP

Why give IP fabrics its own chapter?

Quite simply, it's extremely flexible with respect to the different topologies that it can support, it brings proven carrier-class Internet scaling architecture into the data center with the ability to scale from a few switches to several thousand while keeping the same underlying principle, and it provides a stable foundation for IP connectivity so you can run virtual overlay networks.

The other reason is that Virtual Chassis Fabric and Junos Fusion are fairly straightforward, and IP fabrics are less plug and play, so they need a little planning in their design to implement, and subsequently need a little more space to explain all of the features and their relevance.

IP Fabrics

IP Fabrics have been popular of late because they provide the best support for virtual servers and their applications, and they offer the ability for those applications to talk to each other at scale via Layer 2. While the virtual server world has been moving at breakneck speed to provide speed and agility, the networking world has been a little slow to respond.

Up until a few years ago, most data center networks were based on the traditional three-tiered approach that had been copied from campus network design. While it's fine when most of the traffic has a north/south profile like a campus network, it's not really suitable when the majority of virtual applications and associated workloads need constant east/west communication. East-west traffic is traffic that occurs within the data center and it dominates in nearly all cases of cloud computing, virtualization, and big data. It is one of the driving forces behind the development of data center fabrics.

Multi-tier network data center architectures were optimized for the older north-south traffic, direct traffic from the data center to the end user, not east-west traffic. So in the old design, Layer 2 VLANs would traverse from the server access switch to the aggregation layer and then potentially up to the core layer as shown in Figure 6.1.

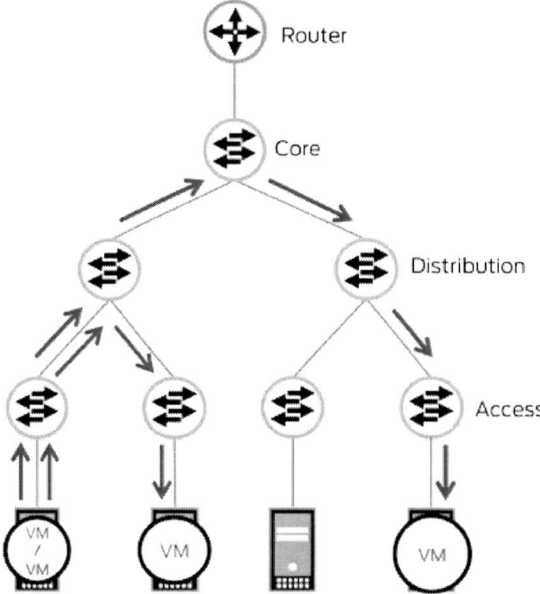

Figure 6.1   Traditional Multi-tier Approach

As you can see in Figure 6.1, this design introduces a fair amount of latency, as the packets need to traverse several hops in order to reach their destination. The more hops required between the different dependent applications, the more those applications are subjected to additional latency, contributing to unpredictable performance and user access to those applications.

This is why fabrics have become so popular; they reduce latency by flattening the architecture so any server node can connect to any other server node with a maximum of two hops, as shown in Figure 6.2. Data center fabric architectures typically use only two tiers of switches as opposed to older data centers that implemented multiple tiered network architectures.

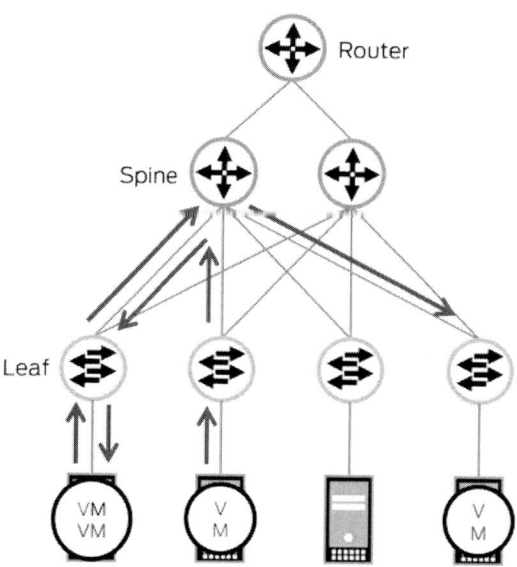

Figure 6.2   IP Fabric's Two Tier Approach

Traffic can be transmitted between server nodes in almost all data center fabric architectures by traversing a set number of switches, which results in extreme efficiency and low latency. The fabric consists of multiple direct paths of high bandwidth, thus removing any potential transmission slowdown caused by network bottlenecks.

Juniper led the innovation of this principle with the release of Q-Fabric in 2010. The idea was to provide single-hop connectivity between servers across a high-speed fabric but with an out-of-band control plane that was connected to every switch device.

An IP Fabric evolves the principles of Q-Fabric to its next logical step by implementing the control plane in software as opposed to a physical out-of-band network and provides the provision for overlay. The majority of IP Fabric architectures are represented by a spine and leaf design in which the fabric mesh incorporates devices on the edge (the leaves) of the fabric and switches on the spine. The spine and leaf model allows for simplified expansion limited only by the number of supported devices and their ports, as shown in Figure 6.3 and as we have covered in previous chapters.

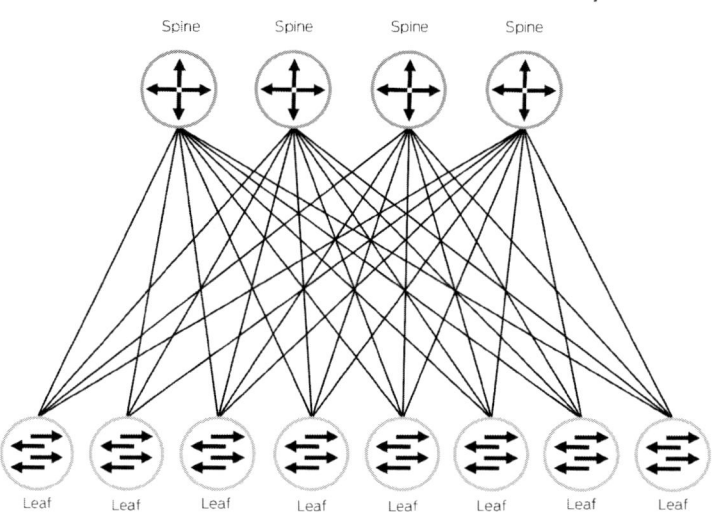

Figure 6.3   IP Fabric Architecture

You can see in Figure 6.3 that the spine layer is made up of four switches. Each leaf has four uplinks, one to each spine. The maximum number of leaves supported in this topology is dictated by the maximum number of ports per a spine. So if our spine switch supports 40 x 40GbE connections, the maximum number of leaf devices would be 40 (though we should allow for onward connectivity at a similar rate to the uplink connectivity, so 36 would be about right).

Clos

Where did the spine and leaf architecture come from? It's based on the principles of a Clos network. Clos networks are named after Bell Labs researcher Charles Clos, who proposed the model in 1952 as a way to overcome the performance and cost-related challenges of electro-mechanical switches then used in telephone networks. Clos used mathematical theory to prove that achieving non-blocking performance in a *switching array* (now known as a fabric) was possible if the switches were organized in a hierarchy.

The design Charles Clos came up with was what he classed as a three stage Clos. A three stage clos is comprised of an ingress, a middle, and an egress, as shown in Figure 6.4.

Chapter 6: IP Fabrics and BGP

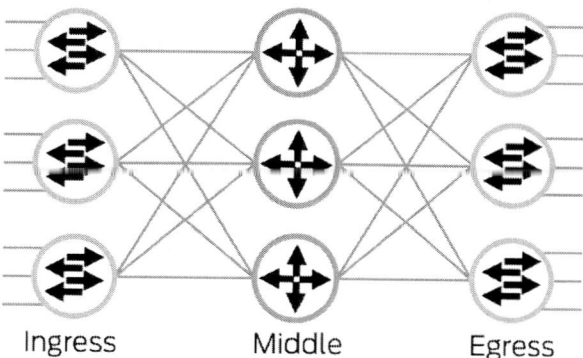

Ingress   Middle   Egress

Figure 6.4   Three Stage Clos (Ingress, Middle, and Egress)

As Figure 6.4 shows, the number of sources which feed into each of the ingress switches is equal to the number of connections connecting to the middle switches and is equal to the number of connections connecting to the egress switches. This provides a non-blocking architecture with no oversubscription. If you now re-name the ingress, middle, and egress, to leaf and spine, you get a Three Stage Clos as shown in Figure 6.5:

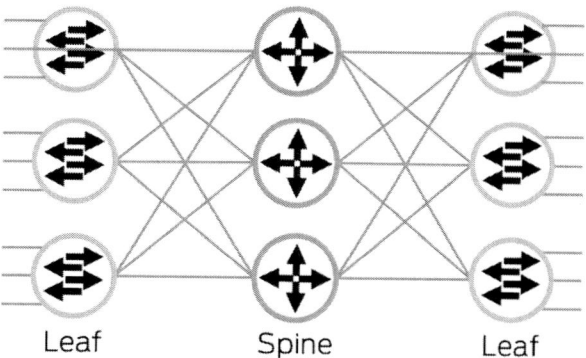

Leaf   Spine   Leaf

Figure 6.5   Three Stage Clos (Leaf, Spine, and Leaf)

Now if you fold this topology in half and turn it on its side, you'll end up with the same spine and leaf architecture as you have seen previously and as outlined in Figure 6.6.

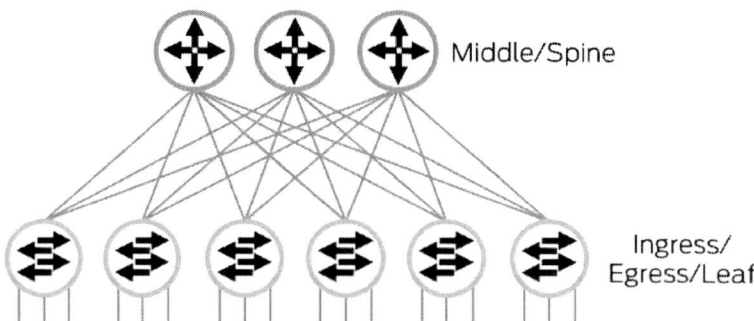

Figure 6.6   Folded Three Stage Clos (Leaf, Spine, and Leaf)

The number of incoming connections is still equal to the number of connections between leaves and the spines and there is still a folded three stage Clos. As discussed later in this chapter, traffic can now be distributed over all available links with no fear of oversubscription.

As more connections are introduced to the leaf layer, our oversubscription ratio increases and you can increase the size of the interconnects to the spines to suit the bandwidth connecting in.

Besides its support for overlay technologies the other benefit of this design is that it offers finely grained failure domains because every switch in the leaf layer is connected to every switch in the spine layer. Thus a failure in one switch in either of the layers does not bring down the entire fabric. As we'll discuss in the next section, you can utilize open standard protocols so you can interoperate with other vendors, which in itself will mean lower CapEx, OpEx, and simpler management. *How does traffic traverse the fabric?* Quite simply, by using Layer 3.

BGP

Layer 3 acts as the control plane in allowing routing information to be distributed to all switches in the fabric. But as you are no doubt aware, there are several different Layer 3 protocols you can choose from. Best practice would argue in favor of any one of the three main open standard protocols: OSFP, IS-IS, or BGP would do the job. Each protocol can essentially advertise routing prefixes, but each protocol varies in terms of scale and features.

Open Shortest Path First (OSPF) and IS-IS use a flooding technique to send updates and other routing information. Creating areas can help limit the amount of flooding, but then you start to lose the benefits of an SPF routing protocol. On the other hand, Border Gateway Protocol (BGP) was created from the ground up to support a large number of prefixes and peering points. The Internet and most service providers are the best examples of BGP as a control plane at scale.

Support for traffic engineering is another requirement that would be useful if you need to steer traffic around a specific spine switch that requires a software upgrade. The limitations with IS-IS and OSFP start to become apparent as these protocols have limited traffic engineering and tagging capabilities, but BGP support for traffic engineering is fundamental to BGP's design and has several features to allowing the tagging of packets:

- Local preference (a metric for internal neighbors to reach external paths – default is 100)
- Multiple exit discriminator (MED) (a metric for external neighbors to reach the AS – default is 0)
- And, extended communities (Routing Tagging)

It's hard to find a reason why you wouldn't use BGP, unless you have had little cause up until now to use BGP in any part of your network. From a campus point of view, many people would consider BGP as a service provider-based protocol, but the fear of learning this complex protocol and how to configure it is being surpassed by automation tools such as OpenClos, which automates the whole process: not only the BGP configuration for each switch, but also the push of the configuration to the switch and bringing the whole fabric up.

Using an automation tool such as OpenClos will still require you to have a basic understanding of BGP. So let's conduct a basic review of BGP basics and BGP design.

BGP Basics

BBGP is an exterior gateway protocol (EGP) used to exchange routing information among routers in different autonomous systems (AS). An AS is a group of routers that are under a single technical administration. BGP routing information includes the complete route to each destination and it uses the routing information to maintain a database of network reachability information, which it exchanges with other BGP systems. BGP uses the network reachability information to construct a graph of AS connectivity, which enables BGP to remove routing loops and enforce policy decisions at the AS level.

BGP uses TCP as its transport protocol, using port 179 for establishing connections. The reliable transport protocol eliminates the need for BGP to implement update fragmentation, retransmission, acknowledgment, and sequencing.

An AS is a set of routers or switches that are under a single technical administration and normally use a single interior gateway protocol and a common set of metrics to propagate routing information within the set of routers. To other ASs, the AS appears to have a single routing plan and presents a consistent picture of what destinations are reachable through it.

The route to each destination is called the *AS path*, and the additional route information is included in *path attributes*. BGP uses the AS path and the path attributes to completely determine the network topology. Once BGP understands the topology, it can detect and eliminate routing loops and select among groups of routes to enforce administrative preferences and routing policy decisions.

BGP supports two types of exchanges of routing information: exchanges between *different* ASs and exchanges *within a single* AS. When used among ASs, BGP is called external BGP (EBGP). When used within an AS, BGP is called internal BGP (IBGP), which leads us quite nicely in to the next section.

BGP Design

The first question posed by using BGP is which variant to use: IBGP or EBGP. The difference between the two may seem quite small, but those minor differences can lead to major changes in your DC implementation. The first big difference between the two is the way they use autonomous systems or ASs.

In IBGP, all switches in the spine and leaf sit under a single AS, as shown here in Figure 6.7. And in EBGP, each switch within the spine and leaf has its own AS, as shown in Figure 6.8.

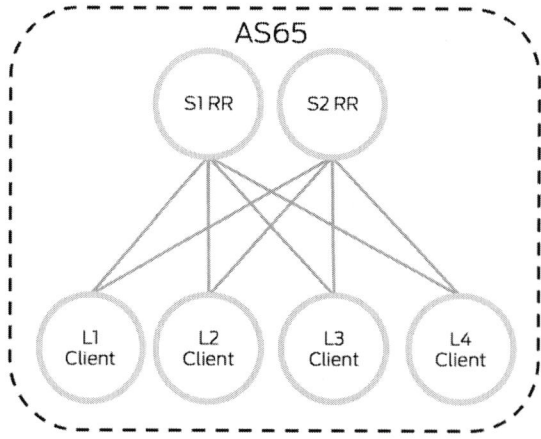

Figure 6.7   IBGP Example

The next issue is how each switch in the fabric distributes prefixes or routes.

IBGP

In BGP you need a full mesh of connected nodes or switches to allow the full distribution of prefixes so each node in the fabric knows of the other, meaning that each node needs to be logically connected to every other node to create a full mesh. But you still need a method of distributing routes between these nodes so they know how to route traffic efficiently. To get address this issue you can use two IBGP options called *confederations* or *route reflectors*.

A confederation is simply a separate internal AS that sits inside your existing single AS. The idea is to break up the internal AS into smaller parts and tie them together with EBGP. Each internal group will still have a full mesh, but it can be as finely grained as you'd like. But in this scenario, using confederations could be a configuration nightmare especially when there's an easier alternative: route reflectors.

A route reflector is an IBGP router that will re-advertise routes to other IBGP routers. This works by creating clusters of IBGP routers, and connecting them with a reflector. So for the DC solution it means the spines become reflectors and the leaves become clients of those reflectors, or route reflector clients.

A reflector will not send every single route; it only sends the best paths to its peers. This presents a problem when you have two or four spines and potentially four routes for traffic to take, from the leaf to the spine. To remove this issue you can enable the *Add-Path* feature on BGP route reflectors so they can advertise four routes of equal measure to the leaf, and traffic can be distributed over all four using *equal-cost multi-path* (ECMP).

ECMP is a solution whereby next-hop packet forwarding to a single destination can occur over *multiple* best paths that tie for top place in routing metric calculations, thus allowing load balancing of packets over those multiple equal paths. So, in normal speak, there are two spine switches and a leaf is connected to both. Normally, IBGP's route calculation would favor one over the other, but you want traffic to be distributed over both, so ECMP would be the normal item to implement. But IBGP doesn't support ECMP as a standard, so you must enable the *add-path* feature we mentioned, which allows the best route to be advertised over *both* links, and then you can use ECMP to distribute the traffic over those two links.

Something to consider when choosing between the two methods is that you have a central point of route management for the fabric, and over time it can become quite large as its holds all the routes for all of the switches in your fabric. As you expand the leaf layer, the route table will get larger and larger and can become quite difficult to manage.

In summary, the spine switches must support BGP route reflection as well as the BGP Add Path feature to meet all of the IP fabric requirements, and your route reflectors may over time become difficult to manage as the configuration gets bigger and bigger – but this allows you to manage the entire IP fabric with a single autonomous system number as opposed to eBGP where you would have to consider the number of ASs you may use.

EBGP

EBGP is easy in comparison to IBGP, because there's no need for BGP route reflection or BGP Add Path to be enabled as ECMP will distribute traffic over all the best paths available and advertised between peers.

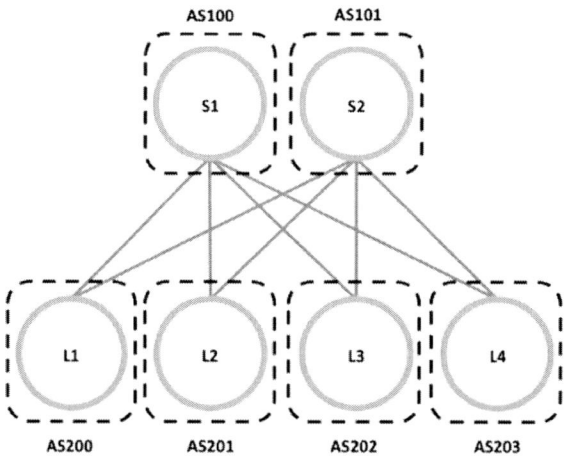

Figure 6.8   **EBGP Example**

The only issue is the number of ASs you might consume with the IP fabric. Each switch has its own BGP AS number, and the BGP private range is 64,512 to 65,535, which leaves you with 1023 BGP autonomous system numbers. If your IP fabric is larger than 1023 switches, you'll need to consider moving into the public BGP autonomous system number range, which I wouldn't advise for an internal data center, or move to 32-bit autonomous system numbers.

Chapter 6: IP Fabrics and BGP

The 32 bit takes the number up to potentially four billion ASs, with the 4,200,000,000 to 4,294,967,294 of the 32-bit range reserved for private addressing, giving you plenty to play with. Note that while Juniper supports 32 bit ASs as standard on its equipment, other vendors may or do not.

Table 6.1 outlines the main points between IBGP and EBGP.

Table 6.1 iBGP and EBGP

IBGP	EBGP
Simple Design	Simple design
IBGP bound to loopbacks	EBGP bound to physical switch
Single BGP ASN	BGP ASN per a switch
Route Reflectors avoids full-mesh peering	Support for traffic engineering
Single routing domain	Distributed routing domains
Add-path required for ECMP	ECMP as standard

BGP and DC1 and DC2

Let's see how BGP ties back into our scenarios for DC1 and DC2.

In DC1 there are five rows of racks with a spine and leaf solution for each row. If we are using EBGP per a row, the BGP design would look like Figure 6.9.

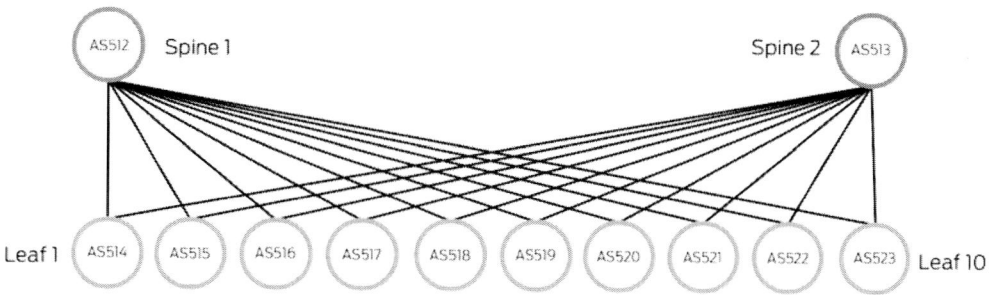

Figure 6.9 EBGP For DC1

As you can see, each switch at both the spine and leaf layer is given its own AS number. This can be repeated for the other rows. So, you could have 64,512 to 523 for row one, and then increase for each device.

With DC2, as we are using an end-of-row solution, the EBGP design would look like Figure 6.10:

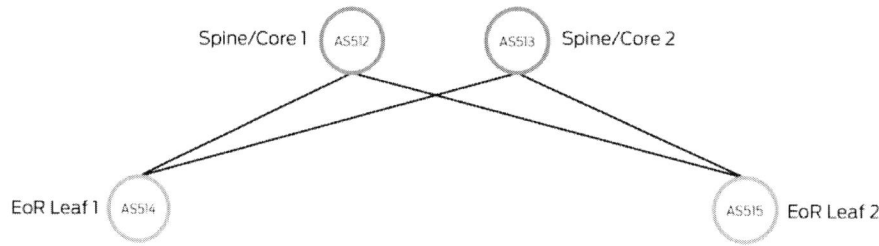

Figure 6.10   EBGP For DC1

Again, as outlined for the DC1 solution, you can use AS64512 and 64513 for row one and then increment by one for each device. If you choose the IBGP method of implementation the design becomes really easy because all you do is assign all of the components to a single AS. This single AS could cover the whole of DC1 and you could have the same approach for DC2 as shown in Figures 6.11 and 6.12.

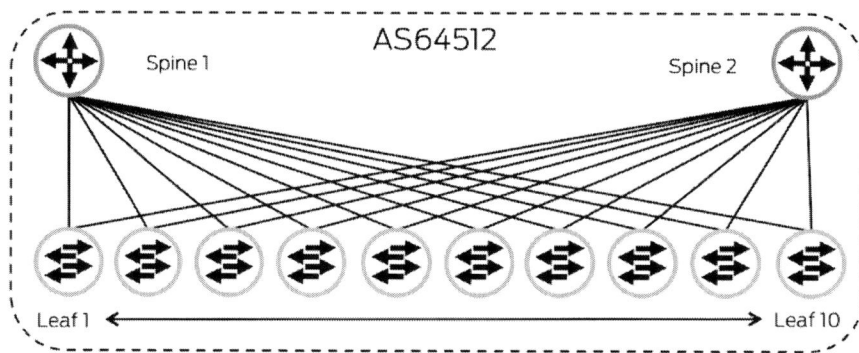

Figure 6.11   IBGP For DC1

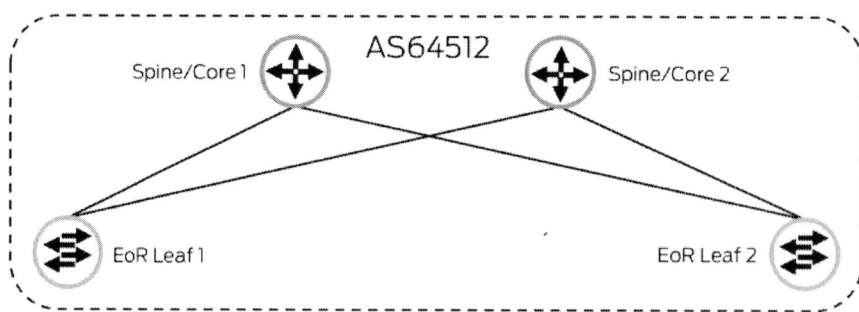

Figure 6.12   IBGP For DC2

Let's move to the support and understanding of overlay networks.

MORE?   An excellent white paper on designing BGP can be found here: http://www.juniper.net/us/en/local/pdf/whitepapers/2000565-en.pdf.

Chapter 7

Overlay Networking

Overlay and *underlay* correspond to the two planes in which communication or data is sent. Fundamentally, an overlay network is a virtual network and an underlay network is a physical network.

An overlay network is built virtually on top of an underlay network using VPNs, or in overlay-speak, using VTEPs (virtual tunnel endpoints). Devices such as virtual servers, virtual switches, and others are connected to each other via these virtual or logical links. Each link then corresponds to a path through the virtual network and is transported over many physical or underlay networks.

As you may be aware, this decoupling of the virtual from the physical enables faster provision of a comprehensive virtual network for the communication between different virtual servers without having to configure, or re-configure, the physical devices that the virtual traffic will traverse.

The benefit for the underlay is simplicity. Because all virtual communication is encapsulated in IP the underlay just needs to transport simple IP data. So you can architect the underlying physical network for simplicity, resiliency, and scale, as we have in the previous chapters, while pushing most of the complexity to the virtual overlay devices and servers.

Tunneling Protocols

So why do we *need* overlay networking?

Where previously one application would be run on one physical server, you can now carve up the processing and memory of a physical server to be able to run multiple virtual servers, thus reducing the number of physical servers you need while increasing the productivity of those same servers. Your average physical server now consists of a *hypervisor*, or VM monitor, that can be a piece of software or firmware that creates and runs multiple VMs.

A computer on which a hypervisor is running one or more VMs is defined as a *host machine*, and each virtual machine is called a *guest machine*. The hypervisor presents the guest operating systems with a virtual operating platform and manages the execution of the guest operating systems. Multiple instances of a variety of operating systems can then share the virtualized hardware resources.

The applications that run on these VMs need to communicate with each other and in general the communication is Layer 2. *But why go to the trouble of an overlay if all they need to do is talk to each other on the same Layer 2 domain?*

Overlay networking is a way to view the network as secondary to the application. With overlay networks you're managing from the application down rather than from the network up because you want to architect that the application gets the services and support from the network to be able to deliver quickly and efficiently. VLANs are a network-imposed solution with limitations, such as the number you can have on a single switch or in a data center. A Layer 2 overlay technology such as a Virtual Extensible LAN (VXLAN) removes those constraints, allowing your server team to implement the network element and bring the application to the user in a manner consistently faster than before. From a network point of view, you're not redundant in this process, but your concern is the Layer 3 element, which is presented to you by the encapsulated protocol.

So, to transport traffic between the different VMs on different physical hardware, you generally use virtual tunnels. These VTEPs typically reside in hypervisor hosts, such as VMware Hypervisor hosts, or kernel-based virtual machine (KVM) hosts, or they can even reside on the switches themselves. Each VTEP has two interfaces: a switching interface that faces the VMs in the host and provides communication between VMs on the local LAN segment, and an IP interface that faces the Layer 3 network. Each VTEP has a unique IP address that is used for routing the UDP packets between VTEPs.

So within each hypervisor, the VMs have the ability to communicate with each other on the same Layer 2 segment through the use of a virtual switch or vSwitch, but if they need to talk to another VM located on another host, they need to traverse the Layer 3 underlay network, which is where the VTEP is required and a protocol is used to encapsulate Layer 2 traffic inside Layer 3 in order to pass it over the Layer 3 underlay. As such, there are a few options.

Tunnel Encapsulation Protocols

There are a number of tunneling/encapsulation protocols that can be used to create overlays in the data center. Network Virtualization using Generic Routing Encapsulation (NVGRE) uses the same principle as in all of the encapsulation overlay protocols, namely it tries to remove the limitation that comes with scaling large Layer 2 networks by encapsulating the Layer 2 packets in a GRE tunnel. Its main sponsor was Microsoft, but they now support VXLAN.

Another option is Stateless Transport Tunneling (STT), an encapsulation mechanism used by VMware mostly for communication between server-based vSwitches. While STT is likely to be more efficient than either VXLAN or NVGRE for the transfer of large amounts of information, it carries more overhead than either VXLAN or NVGRE, with additional header information for smaller packets. Outside of VMware, it's hard to find. And, VMware also supports VXLAN.

You also have the option of MPLS-over-MPLS, or MPLS-over-UDP, but for the sake of brevity, let's assume VXLAN is our preferred tunneling protocol as it is currently the most popular.

VXLAN encapsulates Layer 2 Ethernet frames in Layer 3 UDP packets, enabling the virtualization of Layer 2 subnets, or segments, that can span a physical Layer 3 network.

To explain how VXLAN works, you need to understand two components:

- VXLAN Network ID or *VNI*
- And VXLAN tunnel Endpoint or *VTEP*.

A VNI is similar to an 802.1Q VLAN ID in that it acts as the unique identification of that Layer 2 domain/subnet or segment and allows all VMs within that VNI to communicate with each other.

As noted earlier, the main limitation with traditional VLANs is the number of VLANs supported (4094), due to VLAN packet encapsulation only having a 12-bit ID space, which can only allow 4094.

This limitation becomes apparent when you start to scale your data center to support multiple customers; these customers want to have multiple Layer 2 domains to host their applications, and they want these applications to be active all the time, which means you may need larger facilities to support these requirements. This is what is classed as *multitenancy*.

To get around this issue, VXLAN VNI has a 24-bit length, which means it can provide up to 16M unique L2 IDs thus supporting a considerably larger number of L2 domain and subnets, and removing any scaling and overlap concerns that would have been present using VLANS.

The second element to understand is the VXLAN tunnel endpoint (VTEP), that preforms the encapsulation and decapsulation of packets to travel over the Layer 3 fabric.

VTEPs typically reside within the hypervisor hosts. Each VTEP has two interfaces. One is a switching interface that faces the VMs in the host and provides communication between VMs on the local LAN segment. The other is an IP interface that faces the Layer 3 network. Each VTEP has a unique IP address that is used for routing the UDP packets between VTEPs.

A quick walkthrough might help clarify things, as shown in Figure 7.1.

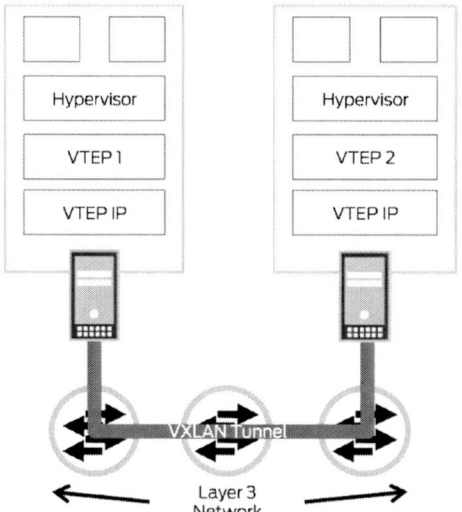

Figure 7.1   A Walkthrough of VTEP

As shown in Figure 7.1, VTEP1 receives an Ethernet frame from VM1, which needs to go to VM3. Both VM1 and VM3 sit within the same VNI, and as such, the forwarding table for that Layer 2 domain has the MAC address for VM3, and which VTEP to pass the packet over. VTEP1 then adds a VXLAN header that contains the VNI to the Ethernet frame, encapsulates the frame in a Layer 3 UDP packet, and routes the packet through to VTEP1 to VTEP 2 over the Layer 3 network.

VTEP2 decapsulates the original Ethernet frame and forwards it to VM3. VM1 and VM3 are completely unaware of the VXLAN tunnel and the Layer 3 network between them. As far as VM1 and VM3 are concerned they could be sitting on the same server, or on different servers within the same data center or in two different data centers. To the VMs the process is transparent; they just sit on the same Layer 2 domain.

To provide a little more context, the packet diagram shown in Figure 7.2 provides some more detail about the packet structure, which will become more relevant when we go through a larger packet walk across a data center network.

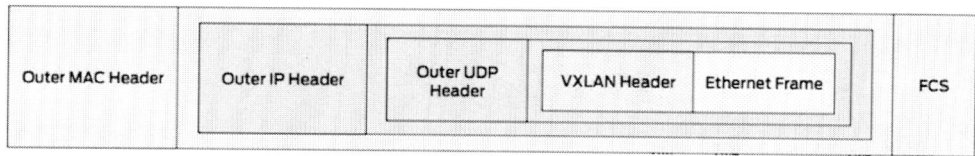

Figure 7.2   Packet Diagram for VTEP

You can see in Figure 7.2 that the original Ethernet frame consists of the source and destination MAC addresses, Ethernet type, and an optional IEEE 802.1q header (VLAN ID). When this Ethernet frame is encapsulated using VXLAN, VXLAN adds these additional elements:

- A VXLAN header that comprises of an 8-byte (64-bit) field which includes the following two fields:
    - Flags: 8 bits in length
    - VNI: A 24-bit value that provides a unique identifier for the individual VXLAN segment.
- Outer UDP Header: The source port in the outer UDP header is dynamically assigned by the originating VTEP and the destination port is typically the well-known UDP port 4789.

- Outer IP Header: The outer IP header has a source IP address of the source VTEP associated with the inner frame source (that could be the VM or a physical server). The outer destination IP address is the IP address of the destination VTEP that corresponds to the inner frame destination.

- Outer Ethernet Header: This has a source MAC address of the VTEP associated with the inner frame source. The destination MAC address is the MAC address of the switching next-hop to reach the destination VTEP.

- Frame check sequence (FCS): New FCS for the outer Ethernet frame.

In total, VXLAN encapsulation adds between 50 and 54 additional bytes of header information to the original Ethernet frame. Because this can result in Ethernet frames that exceed the default 1514 byte MTU, best practice is to implement jumbo frames throughout the network.

MORE?   For a very detailed review of VXLAN, please refer to this IETF draft: https://tools.ietf.org/html/draft-mahalingam-dutt-dcops-vxlan-00.

Packet Walkthrough Using VXLAN

Let's provide a packet walkthrough of the how a packet generated in a VM traverses the network and the processes in place. These steps are numbered below and are illustrated in Figure 7.3:

1. VM1 has a MAC address of 00:00:00:00:00:01 and an IP address of 10.10.10.1 and wants to send traffic to VM2.

2. This traffic is generated on VLAN 10 in the hypervisor with the source MAC and IP and destination MAC and IP (Grey Box).

3. Host A (Hypervisor) encapsulates the original Ethernet Frame along with the payload in to a VXLAN header (light blue) and assigns a VNI of 1001 to act as the ID for that VXLAN. It then creates a VTEP source IP address and destination IP address of the other end of the VTEP, which will be on host B in the Outer IP header (orange). This is where the control plane protocol becomes active as the learning mechanism that allows the VTEP to discover its destination, which is covered in the next section, *Layer 2 Learning*.

4. The packet is then routed across the IP fabric the same as any other packet, as the outer packet details are same IP details as the fabric.

5. As above

6. As above

Chapter 7: Overlay Networking

7. The VTEP-B (Host-B) receives the packet and removes the VXLAN header and forwards the original Ethernet frame.

8. The packet hits the VTEP endpoint and it strips the VXLAN header and switches the original frame towards VM2.

9. The original frame is now just a native Layer 2 frame with payload as was transmitted by VM1.

10. VM2 receives the original frame as if it was on the same VLAN as VM1.

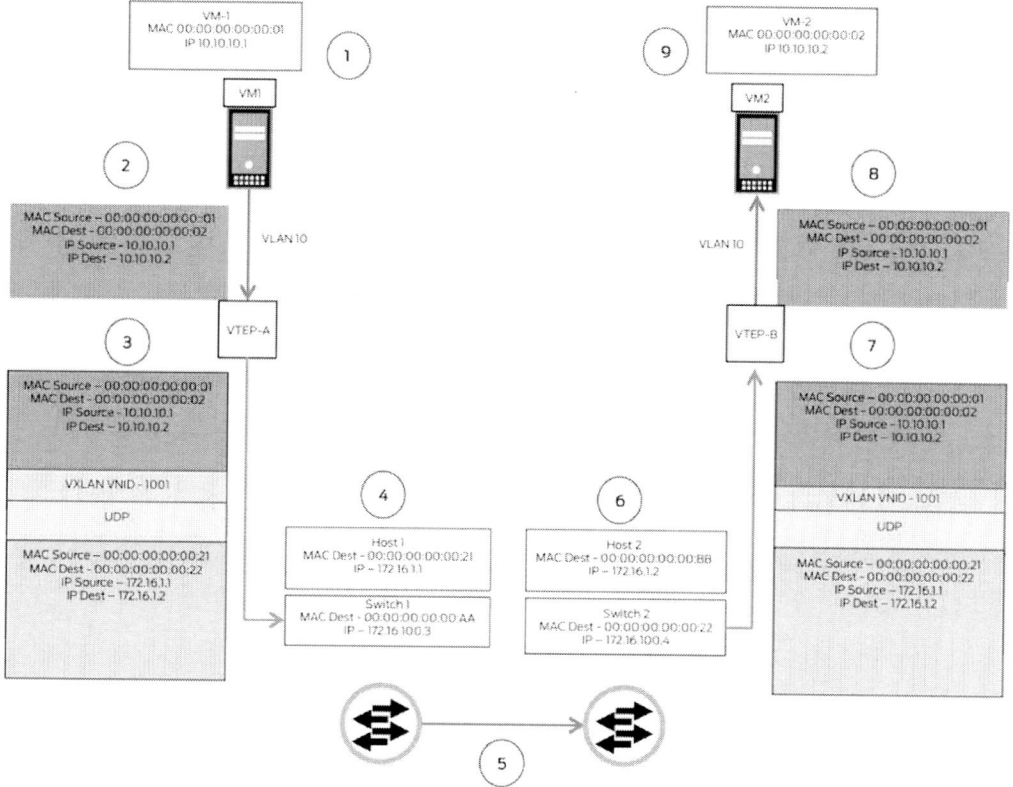

Figure 7.3   A Packet Walkthrough Using VXLAN

NOTE   Ideally, as a best practice, you start VNI numbering from 4K/5K+, for example, VLAN 100 -> VNI 4000 or 5000. However, it doesn't prevent you from configuring VLAN 100 -> VNI 1001, as shown in Figure 7.3.

The steps in Figure 7.3 could easily apply to both a VTEP termination within the hypervisor as well as a VTEP termination in a switch. That's because VTEP endpoints can be located within the hardware of the switch as well as within a VM, due to the simple fact that data centers run a lot of non-virtualized or *bare metal servers* (BMS), which don't have native support for VXLAN.

By placing VTEP endpoints so that they reside on the switches that BMS servers attach to, you can allow the switch to act as a gateway between the virtualized and non-virtualized, thus allowing traffic to move between the two different data planes as if they were connected to the same VLAN, as shown in Figure 7.4.

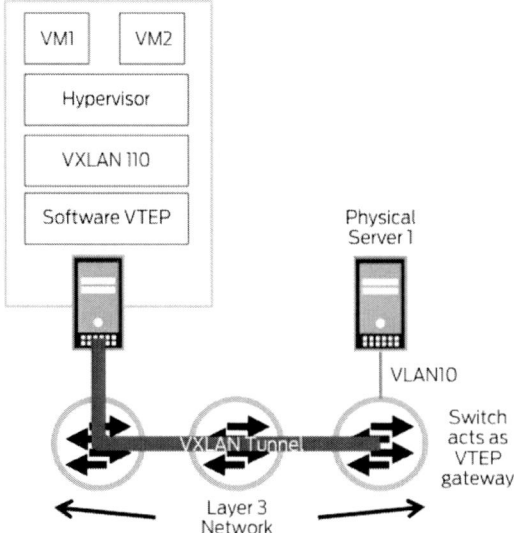

Figure 7.4   VTEP on a Switch Acting as a Gateway

Figure 7.4 shows the two VMs that reside in VLAN10 are encapsulated to VXLAN 110, which is transported across the Layer 3 network, but the VTEP is terminated in the switches hardware. So the VTEP is associated with the interface that connects to the physical server, which is configured for VLAN10, and from the point of view of both the physical and virtual servers, they all reside on VLAN10.

Support for this feature is standard across both switches and routers from Juniper Networks.

Layer 2 Learning

To allow VMs and BMS servers to communicate with each other there has to be a learning mechanism in place (with associated tables) that maps the MAC addresses of VMs and BMSs to specific VTEPs and maintains that mapping.

Let's start with the data plane first. VXLAN as a standard doesn't include a control plane mechanism for VTEPs to share the addresses that they have discovered in the network, but it does include a mechanism that is very similar to the way traditional Ethernet learns MAC addresses. Whenever a VTEP receives a VXLAN packet, it records the IP address of the source VTEP, the MAC address of the VM, and the VNI to its forwarding table. So when a VTEP receives an Ethernet frame for that destination VM server on its VNI segment, it is ready to encapsulate that packet in a VXLAN header and push it towards that VTEP.

If a VTEP receives a packet destined for a VM with an unknown address, it will flood and learn like a traditional Ethernet switch to see if someone else knows the destination MAC address. But, to stop unnecessary flooding of traffic, each VNI is assigned to a multicast group, so the flood and learn process is limited to all of the VTEPs in that VNI's multicast group.

A Packet Walkthrough of VTEP Flood and Learn

The next packet walkthrough will hopefully make the flooding and learning process a little clearer.

As an example, let's suppose that VM1 in Figure 7.5 wants to send a packet to VM2 at IP address 192.168.0.11 but does not have VM2's MAC address. Both VMs reside in VNI 100, which has been assigned to multicast group 239.1.1.100. The sequence follows these steps:

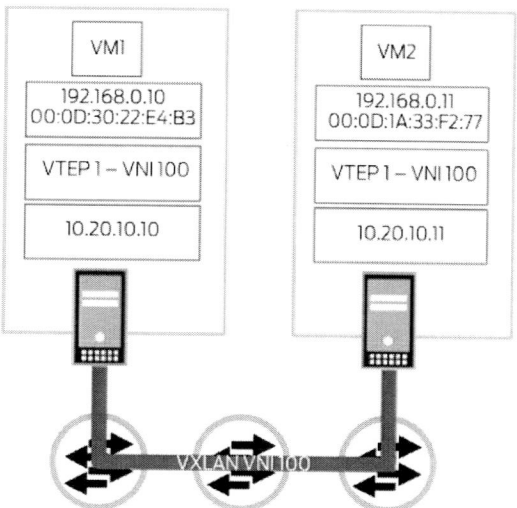

Figure 7.5   VM1 Sends Packets to VM2

1. VM1 sends an ARP packet requesting the MAC address associated with 192.168.0.11.

2. VTEP1 receives this ARP packet. It encapsulates this ARP request into a multicast packet and addresses the packet to the multicast group 239.1.1.100.

3. All VTEPs in multicast group 239.1.1.100 receive the packet. They decapsulate it and check the VNI in the VXLAN header. If the VNI for a local VXLAN segment is 100, the VTEPs forward the original ARP packet to that VXLAN segment. Otherwise, they drop the packet. The VTEPs also add the mapping of the IP address of VTEP1 to the MAC address of VM1 to their local VXLAN tables.

4. When VM2 receives the ARP packet from VTEP2, it responds with its MAC address.

5. VTEP2 encapsulates the response in a unicast IP packet and sends it to VTEP1.

6. VTEP1 receives the ARP packet, decapsulates it, and passes it on to VM1. VTEP1 now stores the mapping of the VTEP2 IP address and the VM2 MAC address in its VXLAN mapping table.

At this point, all relevant MAC addresses have been learned, and VM1 and VM2 can communicate directly via unicast in the future.

Typically, to reduce unnecessary flooding of packets, administrators assign each VNI to its own multicast group. However, there is no requirement that each VNI have its own multicast group – you can assign multiple VNIs to a single multicast group. Isolation of the VXLAN segments is maintained in this case because the VTEP always checks the VNI before it forwards decapsulated packets to a VXLAN segment.

Before moving on to the control plane, there is one aspect that is worth covering: Layer 3 routing for VXLAN because the subject comes up quite often due to differences in support for this feature within different platforms.

VXLAN Routing

At its most basic, VXLAN routing is the ability for one VLAN to talk to another VLAN. To allow this to happen, you need a Layer 3 gateway. It's the same in an overlay network, but when a VXLAN VNI needs to talk to another VXLAN VNI, you need to route between them and you need a Layer 3 gateway.

Juniper prefers to implement VXLAN routing natively in hardware as opposed to either using a multi-stage solution or cabling, either internally or externally, that recirculates the packets in and out of a switch in order to achieve the same process. If you take the spine and leaf model from previous chapters, Layer 3 VXLAN routing can be done at both the spine and leaf layers. In the past, this hasn't been possible at the leaf layer due to limitations with merchant silicon, but those limitations have now been removed, thus allowing routing on a top-of-rack that sits at an affordable price point. Spine layer VXLAN routing has been supported for awhile now in the QFX10000 Series, the MX Series, or the EX9200 Series – all of which use Juniper silicon, which doesn't have those limitations.

The process for routing VXLAN is the same at either the leaf or the spine. Let's quickly walk a packet through the process, beginning with Figure 7.6.

Using the exploded diagram of a single switch in Figure 7.6, there is a server attached to this QFX switch; this server is in VLAN 100 with an IP address of 10.1.100.10 and a gateway of 10.1.100.1. It needs to send a packet to another server on VLAN 101 with an IP address of 10.1.101.10.

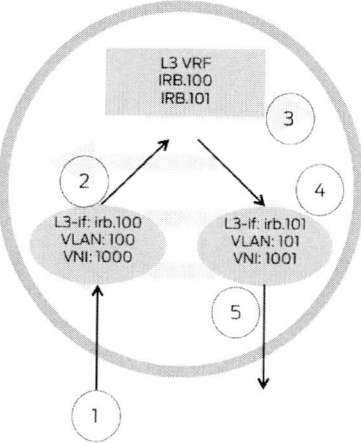

Figure 7.6   Packet Walkthrough of VXLAN Routing

Configured on the switch is a VTEP with the VLAN of 100, a VNI of 1000, and a Layer 3 IRB (integrated routing and bridging) of 100. On the same switch there is also another VTEP with a VLAN of 101, a VNI of 1001, and its own IRB of 101, which ties in to our destination server. Finally there is a secondary Layer 3 virtual routing and forwarding (VRF) that the two VNIs connect and where the routing is done.

1. The QFX switch receives the VXLAN packet with the outer destination IP of its own VTEP. It decapsulates the VXLAN, which leaves a native packet.

2. The QFX switch does a lookup on the destination MAC, which is the local IRB VIP MAC.

3. Another Layer 3 lookup is done inside the L3 VRF routing table.

4. An ARP lookup for 10.1.101.10 (the IP address of our destination packet). If it already exists then destination MAC is resolved. If ARP does not exist it will be resolved by looking at the MAC table of the other VNI.

5. The QFX10000 switch then generates a new Layer 2 header with the destination MAC for 10.1.101.10 (the destination server) and then forwards the encapsulated VXLAN packet to the remote VTEP.

That, in a nutshell, is how Juniper routes between VXLANs on a single switch in the same PFE/ASIC. It's good to know. Now let's move on to the control plane.

IMPORTANT   When you need detailed or up-to-date information on any aspect of this fundamentals book, start at Juniper's Tech Library where all the products, protocols, and configurations can be found: http://www.juniper.net/documentation. The data sheets for all the Juniper devices mentioned in this *Day One* book can be found on their specific product pages at http://www.juniper.net/us/en/products-services/.

Applying What You Have Learned to Your Design

So far we've covered the breakdown of VXLAN and how a packet traverses the network, but how does this apply to the DC1 and DC2 scenario designs? Starting with DC1 if you were to select QFX5100 Series switches you can support all of the elements outlined here with the exception of VXLAN routing. For VXLAN routing, you would need to pass those packets to the spine layer, which would no doubt be a QFX10000 Series. The other option is to implement the newer QFX5110 series, which does support native VXLAN routing.

In DC2, because a QFX10000 Series chassis was specified as the end-of-row devices, VXLAN routing is supported as is VXLAN VTEP termination in hardware. In both cases this means that both of the data center designs support overlay networking from day one.

This leads to the next method of Layer 2 learning via the control plane, which is divided into two elements: a controller-based Layer 2 control plane and going controller-less.

Chapter 8 covers controller-based solutions including Juniper Contrail and VMware's NSX, while Chapter 9 covers EVPN, which the author would argue is the perfect controller-less based protocol for data centers.

Chapter 8

Controllers

The overlay in data centers can either be constructed by a controller or independently by the network nodes. In a controller-based solution, a central brain such as Juniper Contrail or VMware's NSX solution holds the Layer 2 tables and knows how to reach all of the elements in the virtual network, as shown in Figure 8.1. In a controller-less based solution, you are reliant on a protocol to distribute from one point to another.

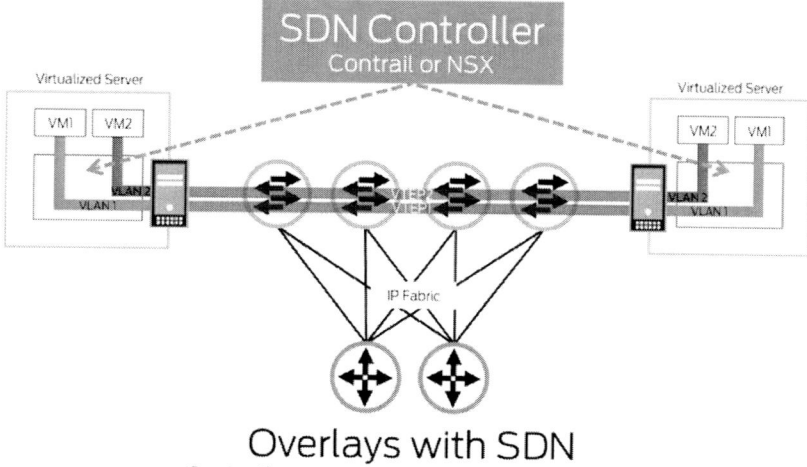

Figure 8.1　A Controller Run Data Center

When a VM needs to send traffic to another VM somewhere else in the data center that it doesn't know how to get to, it does a lookup via a vSwitch or vRouter that resides in the hypervisor of that server. The vRouter (same as a vSwitch) then performs a lookup on its central controller and receives the routes that allow a path to be constructed across the IP fabric – allowing those two VMs to talk to each other. The benefit of this solution is that it's very dynamic and removes the need to configure any network elements, as they just need to route traffic at the IP layer.

It also means that the same controller can configure the switches in the path via protocols such as Open vSwitch Database (OVSDB), allow the MAC routes learned in the physical layer to be passed to the controller, and allow the controller to distribute learned forwarding routes into the physical layer.

So how does a controller like Contrail work to support its traffic solutions?

First, let's quickly review how a controller-less network uses an underlying control plane protocol, such as EVPN, to provide Layer 2 MAC reachability, because EVPN is more likely to be configured on the physical network hardware as opposed to the controller-based solution, which sits at the overlay layer. Examine Figure 8.2.

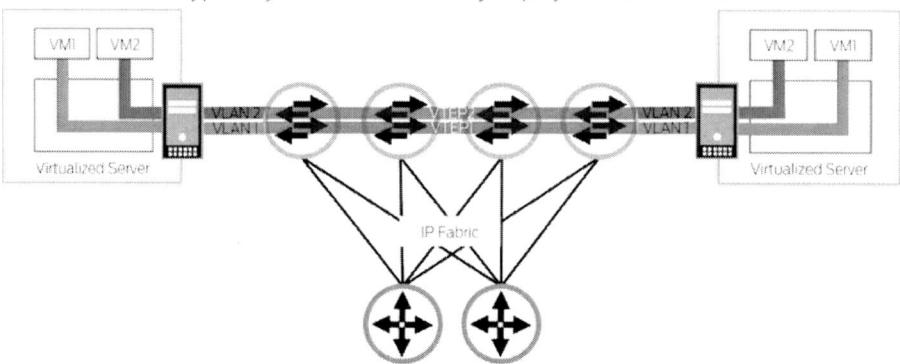

Figure 8.2   A Controller-Less Data Center

As you can see in Figure 8.2, the controller-less network provisions the VTEP network from the network switches. VM-based servers would connect to these switches via standard Layer 2 trunks. While these VTEPs can be controlled via a management platform such as Junos Space, a controller-less solution is a little more static in its implementation and management.

EVPN is covered in detail in Chapter 9; it's a complex subject and requires a diverse protocol in its support for different architectures. Now, let's get back to a controller-based solution. How does it work? Let's look at Juniper Contrail as an example.

Juniper's Controller-Based Solution: Contrail

Contrail is a simple, open controller-based solution that automates and orchestrates the overlay network. It consists of two main components, the Controller and the vRouter, and takes normal networking terms such as MPLSoGRE, MPLSoUDP, and VXLAN with BGP and applies them to the virtual world.

The Contrail controller is a logically centralized but physically distributed (distributable) software-defined networking (SDN) controller, responsible for providing the management, control, and analytics functions for the overlay network.

The Contrail vRouter acts as the local forwarding plane running in the hypervisor of a virtualized server. It takes the networking principles from physical routers and switches in a data center and puts them into a virtual overlay network hosted in the virtualized network. (The vRouter is very similar to a vSwitch but it also provides additional higher layer services such as routing and security, hence the vRouter name.)

The Controller provides the centralized control plane and management plane of the system and orchestrates the vRouters, which forward the traffic. The physical underlay network is responsible for providing unicast IP connectivity from any physical device (server, storage device, router, or switch) to any other physical device. The vRouters running in the hypervisors of the virtualized servers create a virtual overlay network on top of this physical underlay network using a mesh of dynamic "tunnels" among themselves. In the case of Contrail, these overlay tunnels can be MPLS over GRE/UDP tunnels, or VXLAN tunnels, which means support for both Layer 3 overlays using the same protocols as standard MPLS and Layer 2 VXLAN with EVPN.

The underlay physical routers and switches do not contain any state relating to MAC addresses, IP address, or policies for VMs. The forwarding tables of the underlay physical routers and switches only contain the IP prefixes or MAC addresses of the physical servers.

The vRouters, on the other hand, contain a separate forwarding table for each virtual network. That forwarding table contains the IP prefixes to support Layer 3 overlay networks or the MAC addresses for Layer 2 overlays of the VMs. Because of the central controller, no single vRouter needs to contain all of the addressing for all the VMs in the entire data center. Figure 8.3 illustrates a controller-based solution using Juniper Contrail.

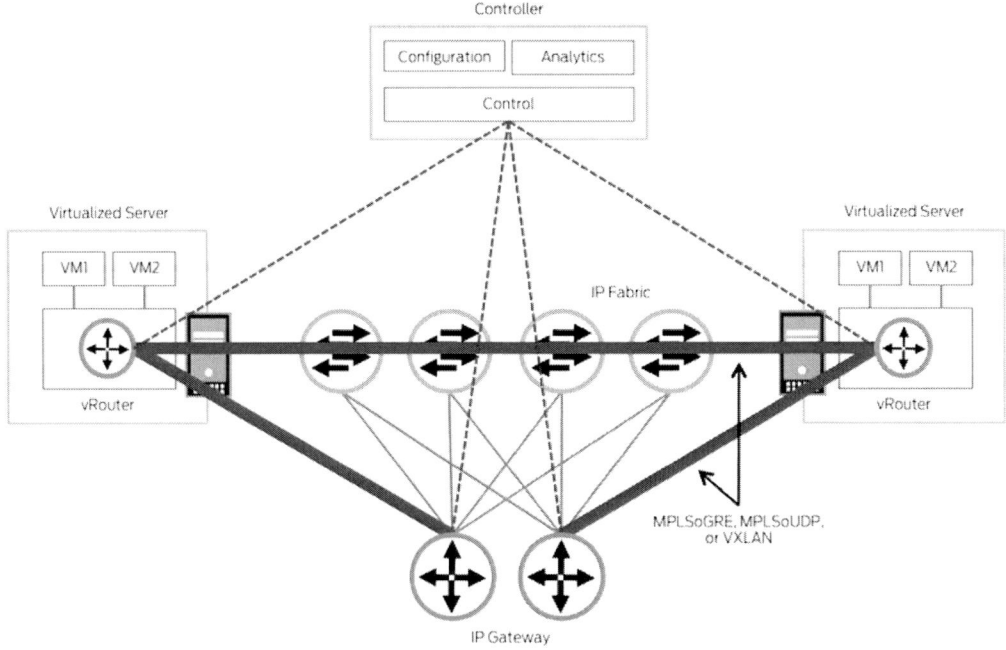

Figure 8.3　A Controller-Based Solution Using Juniper Contrail

Before examining the vRouter and controller in more depth, let's quickly cover three aspects of the Contrail system that make the solution work: configuration, control, and analytics, all of which are present in both the vRouters and controller.

- *Configuration*: The configuration component keeps an active copy of the configuration state, present in each vRouter and in the controller.

- *Control*: The control component implements a logically-centralized control plane that is responsible for maintaining network state. This control function interacts with each vRouter and with other network elements, such as gateways, to ensure that network state is consistent.

- *Analytics*: The analytics component collects, stores, correlates, and analyzes information from network elements, virtual or physical. This information includes statistics, logs, events, and errors. This information aids in troubleshooting and real-time event data for capacity planning.

Contrail Controller

From the Controller's point of view, each of the three elements: configuration, control, and analytics, becomes its own node. So there's a control node, a configuration node, and an analytics node. Each of these logical nodes runs on an X86 processor that may be on a separate physical server or running as a VM, or indeed, all running on a single server in your lab. As all nodes run in an active/active configuration, you can run multiple instances of these nodes so no one node becomes a bottleneck, and that allows you to scale out the solution and provide redundancy. These nodes are interconnected to each other, with the control nodes being the nodes that the vRouters interact with as shown in Figure 8.4.

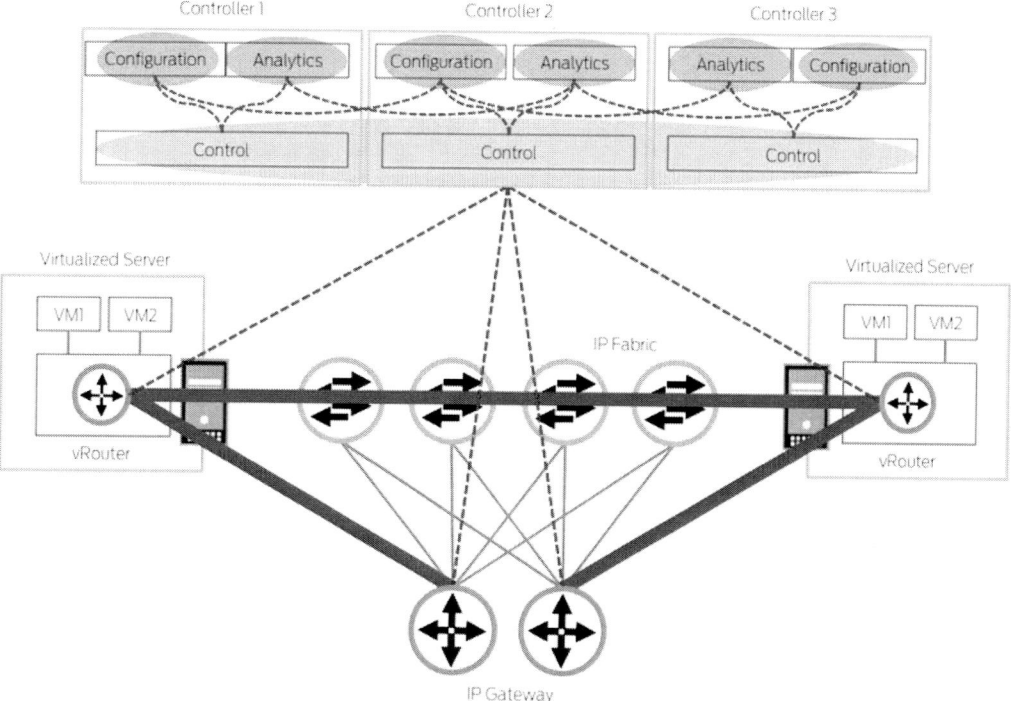

Figure 8.4   Contrail Controller

Each vRouter connects to three or more controller nodes (as shown in Figure 8.4) where all the nodes are active-active. Think of this as a collection of control nodes where the vRouter receives all its state (routes, routing instance configuration, etc.) from each of these control nodes. The vRouter then makes a local decision about which copy of the control state to use – it's similar to how a BGP PE router receives multiple copies of the same route (one from each BGP neighbor) and makes a local best route selection. The information is then added to the local table until the controller advertises a better route.

If a control node fails, the vRouter agent will notice that the connection to that control node is lost. The vRouter agent will flush all routes that it received from the failed control node. It already has a redundant copy of all the states from the other control node. The vRouter can locally and immediately switch over without any need for resynchronization. The vRouter agent will do a discovery for the remaining control nodes to see if a new control node exists to replace the old one. If not it will continue to use the single control node that it knows about until another one recovers.

Contrail vRouter

The vRouter sits within the compute servers hosting your VMs. The standard configuration assumes Linux is the host OS, and KVM is the hypervisor (but other hypervisors are supported). The vRouter is then divided into two functions, the vRouter *forwarding plane* and the vRouter *agent*. The vRouter forwarding plane for Virtio sits in the Linux kernel, but for those running the Data Plane Development Kit (DPDK) support it sits in user space and the vRouter agent is in the local user space as shown in Figure 8.5.

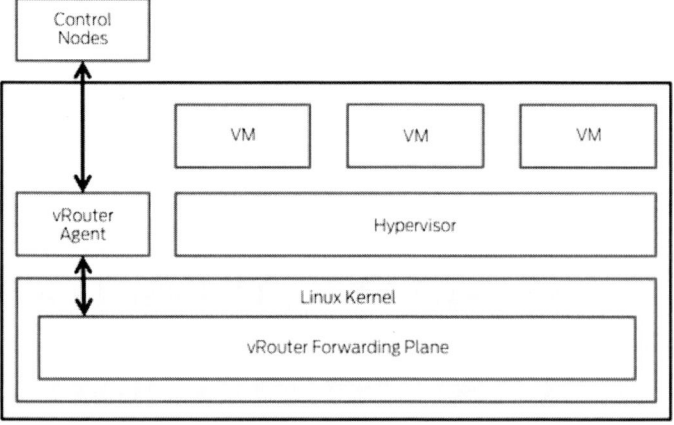

Figure 8.5   Structure of the Contrail vRouter

The vRouter agent connects to the control nodes to receive forwarding information and the vRouter forwarding plane is the virtual router.

The vRouter agent is a user space process running inside Linux. It acts as the local, lightweight control plane, and is responsible for the following functions:

- Exchanging control state such as routes with the Control nodes
- Reporting analytics state such as logs, statistics, and events to the analytics nodes
- Installing routing tables into the forwarding plane
- Discovery of existing VMs and their associated attributes
- Applying policy for the first packet of each new flow and installing a flow entry in the flow table of the forwarding plane
- Proxy DHCP, ARP, DNS, and MDNS

Each vRouter agent is connected to at exactly two control nodes for redundancy in an active-active redundancy model.

As mentioned, the vRouter is a virtual router and runs as a kernel module or in user space depending on the forwarding mechanism (Virtio or DPDk) in Linux and is responsible for the following functions:

- Encapsulating packets and de-encapsulating packets sent and received over the overlay network
- Assigning packets to a routing instance
- Assigning packets received from the overlay network and assigning them to a routing instance based on the MPLS label or virtual network identifier (VNI)
- Doing a lookup of the destination address in the forwarding information base (FIB) and forwarding the packet to the correct destination. The routes may be Layer 3 IP prefixes or Layer 2 MAC addresses. Optionally, when applying forwarding policy using a flow table it matches packets against the flow table and applies the flow actions.

One element of this process that's important to discuss is how you can assign different VMs to different vRouter instances as shown in Figure 8.6. This is relevant in the same way that a VLAN can be assigned to a VXLAN tunnel, and as such, a Layer 2 domain. The principle is the same, but you create separate virtual routers to do the isolation and move it down in to the hypervisor layer, as opposed to being on the switch layer. That means you can have multiple Layer 2 and Layer 3 domains, which will not interact with each other unless configured to do so.

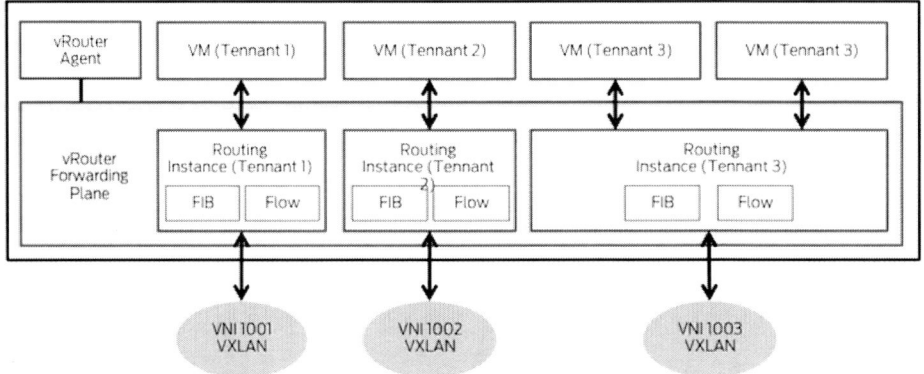

Figure 8.6   Assigning Different VMs to Different vRouters

Where Figure 8.6's detail becomes naturally advantageous is in a multi-tenant environment, where you need to offer multiple VMs and domains but with complete separation and simple centralized control and configuration.

As mentioned previously, Contrail vRouters, and Contrail as a whole, support MPLS over GRE or UDP and VXLAN, but it is worth noting that the selection of which data plane protocol to use is based on a preference order that can be defined during setup, and also takes into account the capabilities of the two endpoints of the tunnel. Either you define the tunnel type or the vRouters can do that based on what the tunnel endpoints support.

So elements covered in Chapter 7 on VXLAN stay the same and you implement Contrail to manage that overlay element. If, on the other hand, you come from an MPLS background, then the support for MPLS is the same as it would be for a MPLS WAN network, but implemented in the data center where the encapsulation method of the packets is MPLS with a MPLS label to act as its ID.

Let's join this all together with a packet walkthrough on how VM1A could talk to VM1B across our fabric.

Packet Walkthrough in a Contrail Solution

In the scenario shown in Figure 8.7, VM1A needs to send packets to VM1B, which is located on a different server in the data center.

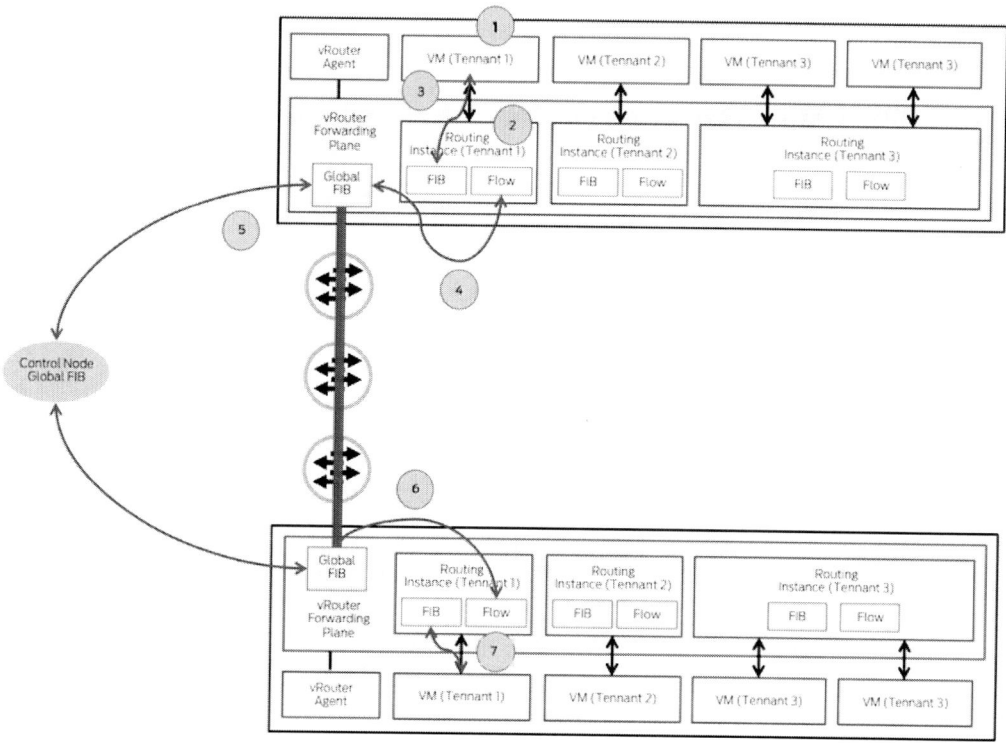

Figure 8.7 **Packet Walkthrough for Contrail vRouter Traffic**

Let's begin with an application sitting within VM1 that wants to communicate with another application within VM2:

1. VM1 has a default route pointing to a local address that resides in the vRouting instance 1, effectively its next-hop address, so it sends an ARP request to that next-hop address.

2. The Routing 1 instance receives the ARP, and the proxy process within the vRouter 1 instance replies.

3. VM1 receives the reply and sends the initial packet through to vRouter 1.

4. The vRouter 1 instance receives the packet and does an initial lookup in its local FIB table. If the route is in the local FIB table, then the packet would be encapsulated and sent on to the next hop, which would be the global FIB table that resides in vRouter 1 (vRouter 1 can

have multiple routing instances). The instances look after their associated VMs and provide local routing and switching between VMs in that instance. If the packet is destined for outside of that instance, if the packet is destined for a node outside the routing instance's domain, then one of three things will happen:

- If a policy exists that says that the destination should be reachable from that routing instance, then a route will be applied in that instance providing the next-hop and label required to reach the destination and normal encap as outlined;
- If there's a default route, the packet will follow that path;
- If nothing is defined, then the packet will be dropped.

5. The vRouter 1 does a lookup of the new destination IP address of the encapsulated packet in its global IP FIB table. If it's present then it will be encapsulated again with the outer IP address of the compute server where the hypervisor resides. It does a lookup in the master global route table, responds back to vRouter 1 with the routes, and vRouter1 updates its tables.

6. The encapsulated packet is now transported over the IP fabric until it gets to compute server 2. It decapsulates the packet and passes it to the vRouter, which does a lookup in its global FIB. It sees that the packet is destined for vRouter instance 1 and passes it to that instance.

7. Finally, vRouter instance 1 receives the packet, decapsulates the packet to expose the inner IP or Layer 2 information, then checks its local FIB to route or switch that packet to the correct VM, and sends it through to that VM.

So, that's Contrail. You'll see similarities with a router that supports multiple VRFs that access a central control plane holding the routing and switching information. It is also similar to BGP routing devices that are clients of a BGP route reflector holding all the routes for that BGP AS.

MORE? For an even more detailed and up-to-date view of Juniper Contrail and its specifications, please refer to its product page on the Juniper web site, with links to papers, documentation, and solutions: http://www.juniper.net/us/en/products-services/sdn/contrail/.

MORE? If you require more detail on how VMWare NSX and Juniper work together to provide a more enterprise oriented solution, refer to the NSX design guide: https://www.vmware.com/files/pdf/products/nsx/vmw-nsx-network-virtualization-design-guide.pdf. And the Juniper version can be found here: https://www.juniper.net/us/en/local/pdf/whitepapers/2000525-en.pdf.

Contrail as a Controller in a Pure Switch Solution

This chapter has been looking at SDN from the point of view of encapsulation from the hypervisor layer. Contrail also supports a dynamic overlay and encapsulation based purely in the switch layer. This is to provide support for BMSs that don't run VM-based services, as well as for virtual servers for which you may not want the encapsulation to happen at that layer, but still want a dynamic central controller for MAC learning and provision.

Contrail achieves this through the use of the Open vSwitch Database Management (OVSDB) Protocol that is supported in all of the QFX switches. The OVSDB protocol is used to configure the top-of-rack switch and to import dynamically-learned addresses from the BMS and virtual servers connected to those switches. Contrail then uses VXLAN encapsulation as the data plane communication across the fabric between the top-of-rack switches.

To implement this overlay, Contrail employs two services: a *top-of-rack services node* (TSN) and a *top-of-rack Agent*. TSN acts as the multicast controller for the top-of-rack switches providing the MAC learning and distribution. The TSN also provides DHCP and DNS services to the BMS or virtual instances running behind top-of-rack switch ports.

The TSN receives all the broadcast packets from the top-of-rack switch, and replicates them to the other switches within the fabric and the required compute nodes in the server cluster. Broadcast packets from the VMs in the server cluster are sent directly from the respective compute nodes to the top-of-rack switch. This allows for a full map of the server and switch topology to be constructed.

As mentioned, TSN can also act as the DHCP server for the BMS or virtual instances, leasing IP addresses to them, along with other DHCP options configured in the system. The TSN also provides a DNS service for the BMS. Multiple TSN nodes can be configured in the system based on the scaling needs of the cluster.

The other service, a top-of-rack agent, is provisioned in the Contrail controller cluster and acts as the OVSDB client for the top-of-rack switch, and all of the OVSDB interactions with the top-of-rack switch are performed by using the top-of-rack agent. The top-of-rack agent programs the different OVSDB tables onto the top-of-rack switch and receives the local unicast table entries from the top-of-rack switch.

The typical practice is to run the top-of-rack agent on the TSN node. In addition to running the different tables, the top-of-rack agent also receives the configuration information for the top-of-rack switch from

Contrail. The top-of-rack agent translates the Contrail configuration to OVSDB and populates the relevant OVSDB table entries in the top-of-rack switch.

Control Plane

At the control plane level we can use EVPN to allow us to contrast multiple virtual networks (if required for, say, a multi-tenant solution). The top-of-rack agent receives the EVPN route entries for the virtual networks in which the top-of-rack switch ports are members, and adds the entries to the unicast remote table in the OVSDB.

MAC addresses learned in the top-of-rack switch for different logical switches (entries from the local table in OVSDB) are propagated to the top-of-rack agent. The top-of-rack agent exports the addresses to the control node in the corresponding EVPN tables, which are further distributed to other controllers and subsequently to compute nodes and other EVPN nodes in the cluster such as gateways for transportation between data centers.

The TSN node receives the replication tree for each virtual network from the control node. It adds the required top-of-rack addresses to the received replication tree, forming its complete replication tree. The other compute nodes receive the replication tree from the control node, whose tree includes the TSN node, thus allowing every device in the fabric a complete view.

Data Plane

In the data plane you can use VXLAN encapsulation (as discussed in pervious chapters). The VTEP for the BMS is on the top-of-rack switch. Unicast traffic from BMS is VXLAN-encapsulated by the top-of-rack switch and forwarded, if the destination MAC address is known within the virtual switch. Unicast traffic from the virtual instances in the Contrail cluster is forwarded to the top-of-rack switch, where VXLAN is terminated and the packet is forwarded to the BMS.

Broadcast traffic from BMS is received by the TSN node which uses the replication tree to flood the broadcast packets across that specific virtual network. Broadcast traffic from the virtual instances in the Contrail cluster is sent to the TSN node, which then replicates the packets to the top-of-rack switches.

DC1 and DC2 Contrail Solutions

Remember the solutions we crafted earlier for DC1 and DC2? Well, both DC1 and DC2 topologies support a controller-based solution using either Contrail or VMware, whereby the VTEP termination can be done either in the hypervisors of servers (KVM or ESXi based), or directly in the switch hardware for BMS-based and HyperV systems. In either case, the topology supports the IP fabric and interaction between the controller-based systems.

Figure 8.8 shows DC1 with a controller acting as the control plane for the Layer 2 virtual networks between the servers.

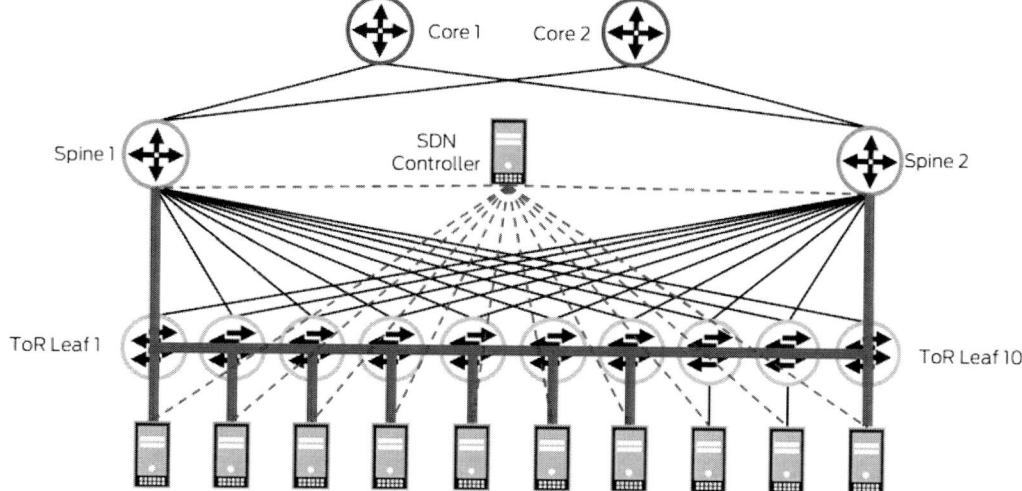

Figure 8.8   DC1 Contrail Solution

The controller's points of control (represented with red dashed lines) attach to the servers where software VTEPs are constructed for the multiple VMs as well as in the switch hardware, where the controller can construct VTEPs and where the spine switches act as gateways between the virtual overlay and wider connectivity all the way up to the core layer (the controller, in both instances, could use the core layer as the gateway if required; it's an option).

Remember that the principles are the same in the DC2 topology; the top-of-rack termination was just moved from the racks to two end-of-row chassis switches. The VTEP termination in hardware is still fully supported as is the software VTEP pass-through to the hypervisor based servers.

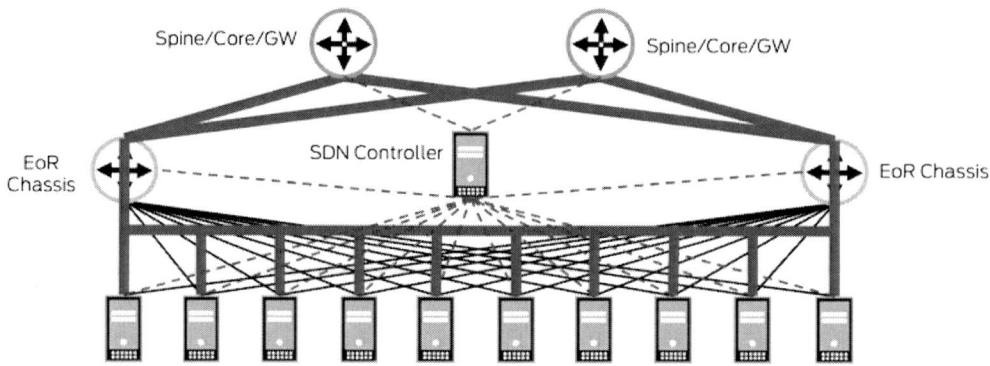

Figure 8.9   DC2 Contrail Solution

You can see in DC2 that traffic is more centralized due to the end-of-row design. IIt also means that the gateway between the wider network and the overlay sits at the spine/core acting as the main aggregation point between all of the rows, and then onward connectivity to the WAN or outside of the data center.

Okay, remember all this because next up is EVPN as a controller-less based solution for supporting overlay networking.

Chapter 9

EVPN Protocol

As mentioned in Chapter 8, the second option for control planes in an overlay network is to remove the controller and use a protocol to provide the MAC learning mechanism for your VXLAN VTEPs.

The choice is somewhat limited to multicast or EVPN. While multicast is a valid option, it is a limited protocol compared to EVPN and the additional topologies EVPN can support. So let's stick with EVPN-VXLAN.

MORE? Note that EVPN addresses lots of different implementations besides Level 2 control plane as outlined in this chapter. For more details on all the different implementations of EVPN look in the Juniper TechLibrary: http://www.juniper.net/techpubs/en_US/junos/topics/concept/evpns-overview.html.

EVPN addresses two issues: the first, as we have discussed, is a MAC learning control plane for overlay networks, and the second is the need for workload mobility. Remember that workloads, or applications, require a Layer 2 domain to interact with each other. That's fine inside a single data center where you can stretch VLANs either in a traditional sense or via an overlay. But in many cases those same workloads need to be present in two (or more) data centers to provide an active/active redundancy to client applications. That means stretching these VLANs over a WAN between the two data centers and making that Layer 2 domain seem as if it is locally present. But that's really the focus of EVPN-VXLAN stitching to EVPN-MPLS. Let's focus on EVPN-VXLAN.

For the past few years you could use VPLS (virtual private LAN service) to stretch that Layer 2 domain between sites. But while VPLS did a good job, like any protocol it also came with limitations regarding: MAC address scaling, support for multicast in a sensible way, multi-homing active/active, transparent customer MAC address transport, faster convergence, and no doubt the largest pain, ease of management.

EVPN attempts to address these issues, but remember that it's still a new protocol and in some cases the standards are still being worked out, which is why you'll see slightly different implementations by different vendors.

EVPN is in the BGP family. It uses multi-protocol BGP for the learning of MAC addresses between switches and routers and allows those MAC addresses to be treated as routes in the BGP table. This means you can use multiple active paths both inside and between data centers without blocking links. But you're not just limited to MAC addresses. You can you use IP addresses plus the MAC address (this forms a ARP entry) to be routed and you can combine them further with a VLAN tag as well.

Given this flexibility for both Layer 2 and Layer 3 addressing, and the fact that you can use a single control plane such as BGP for both the internal network and the external WAN, the benefits of EVPN quickly become apparent.

Before delving into the innards of EVPN, let's sync up and run through some of the terminology and how that terminology applies to a fabric.

Let's start with Figure 9.1, which shows two servers with two VMs per server attached to leaves in a standard spine and leaf topology. Compared to previous diagrams, you should note that that each server is attached to two leafs for resiliency, just as it should be in the real world. The diagram used in Figure 9.1 is used throughout this chapter to build upon EVPN concepts and where they apply.

Starting with the server connection, as shown in Figure 9.2, the server connects to the switch and has a trunk with two VLANs present (VLAN 1 and VLAN 2). In EVPN-speak these two VLANs are classed as *Ethernet Tags*, which is simply the identity of the VLAN, so Ethernet Tag 1 corresponds with VLAN Tag 1 and in EVPN the Ethernet tag *maps* to the VLAN tag.

Chapter 9: EVPN Protocol 105

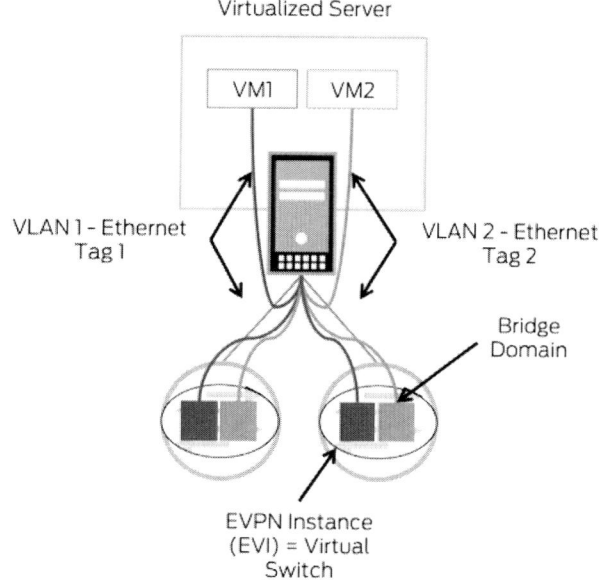

Figure 9.1   **Basic EVPN Topology**

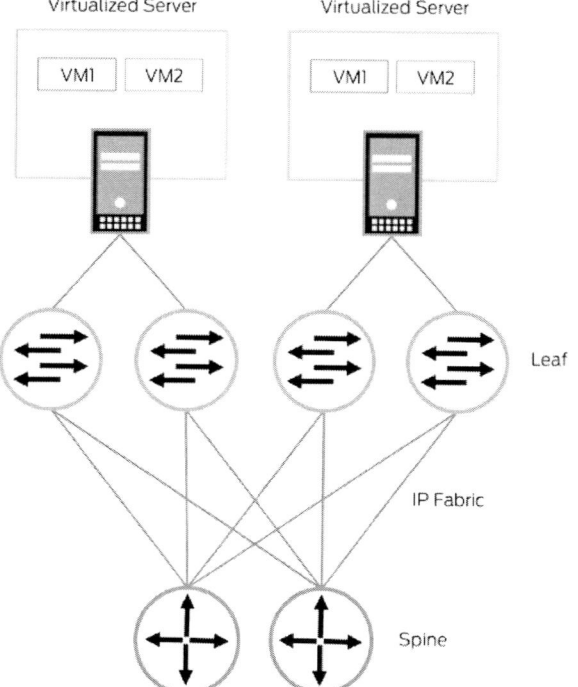

Figure 9.2   **EVPN Tags and Mapping**

Inside each EVI is *MAC-VRF*, which is a virtual MAC table for the forwarding and receiving of MAC addresses within the EVI. You also have an *import* policy and an *export* policy.

The *VRF export policy* for EVPN is a statement configured in the VRF. This statement causes all locally learned MACs to be copied into the VRF table as EVPN *Type 2* routes. Each of the Type 2 routes associated with locally learned MACs will be tagged with the community target of say 1:1, and these tagged routes are then advertised to all switches in the fabric.

The *VRF import policy* statement does the reverse of the export statement to accept routes that are tagged with that target community.

You also have a *route distinguisher* or RD that is assigned to the MAC-VRF, again this is unique, and its ID is advertised into the BGP control plane that runs across the whole of our fabric.

There is a *route target* (RT) *community*. Each EVPN route advertised by a switch in the fabric contains one or more route target communities. These communities are added using VRF export policy or by a configuration, as mentioned earlier. When another switch in the fabric receives a route advertisement from other switches, it determines whether the route target matches one of its local VRF tables. Matching route targets cause the switch to install the route into the VRF table whose configuration matches the route target.

Finally, EVPN gives you the flexibility to support different VLAN mapping options per an EVP instance. These different supported options are classed as *EVPN services*.

VLAN Services

There are three VLAN services with the first one being VLAN-based service as shown in Figure 9.3. With this service a VLAN is mapped to a single EVI and it becomes the EVI for that VLAN across the fabric.

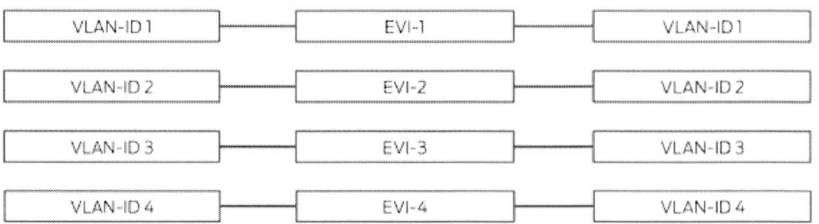

Figure 9.3   **VLAN-Based Service**

This method provides excellent separation on a VLAN-per-VLAN basis and limits the MAC broadcast for each VLAN, but scale and operational overhead are the limiting factors, especially if you want several thousand VLANs per data center and their associated EVIs.

One benefit that is worth considering is something called VLAN manipulation or normalization. This means that you can map the original VLAN to a different VLAN, something you can do with VPLS. An example would be if you had two fabrics in a single data center, with odd numbered VLANs in one fabric and even numbered VLANs in the other. You can map VLAN 1 to EVI-1 and then to, say, VLAN 11 in the other fabric.

Your next VLAN service option, which was outlined in the initial example, is mapping two or more VLANs to a single EVI. This is called *VLAN bundle service*. It means that a group of servers with a series of VLANs can be mapped to a single EVI across the fabric as shown in Figure 9.4. This is useful if you are offering tenant-based services and tenants have overlapping VLANs with other tenants. Providing VLANs with a single EVI means they have a unique RT and RD across the fabric providing complete separation.

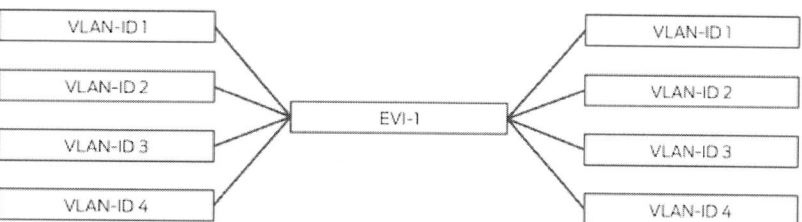

Figure 9.4   VLAN Bundle Service

The benefits here are the efficient way in which you can bundle like VLANs together and operationally make the configuration a lot easier. But traffic flooding will affect every VLAN in the EVI, and you have no support for the VLAN mapping, so you are sharing the EVI with lots of other VLANs.

The last service is called *VLAN aware service* and it allows for multiple VLANs and bridge domains to be mapped to a single EVI, as shown in Figure 9.5. It allows all of the VLANs to share the single EVI but because you have the one-to-one mapping of VLAN to bridge domain, you can assign an ID or label to that bridge domain to provide separation between other VLANs. It also means that flooding only affects the VLAN in which it occurs, as opposed to the bundle service where it affects every VLAN in the EVI.

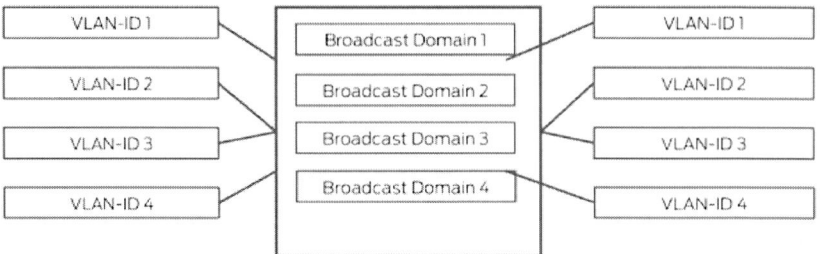

Figure 9.5   VLAN Aware Service

NOTE   At the time of this book's writing, the Juniper's QFX Series currently only supports VLAN Aware and VLAN Bundle. The MX Series and the EX9000 Series support all three.

While you have already read about data plane encapsulation like VXLAN and the different protocols that you can use for the overlay, it's still worth touching upon the ones supported by EVPN.

Data Plane

As shown in Figure 9.6, there are currently five supported data plane technologies for EVPN. They are MPLS, PBB, SST, NVGRE, and VXLAN. All five are encapsulation methods using EVPN and BGP as the common control plane.

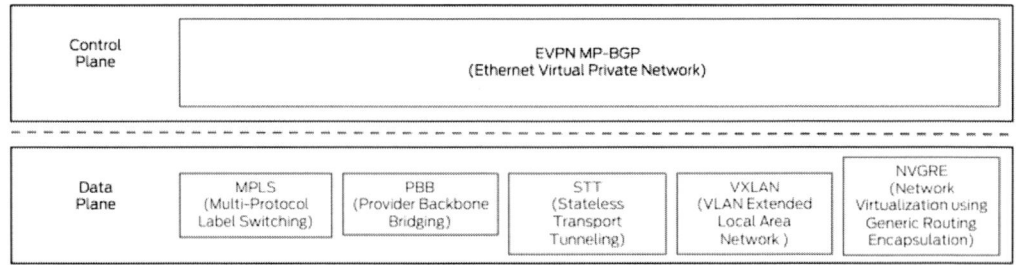

Figure 9.6   EVPN Supported Data Plane Technologies

At the time of publication of this *Day One* book, Juniper supports three forms of EVPN encapsulation: VXLAN, MPLS over MPLS, and MPLS over UDP.

You know that the VXLAN encapsulation method over the fabric uses the concept of VNIs or VXLAN Network IDs, so your VLAN 1 and 2 are assigned VNI-1 and VNI–2.

You should now have two VLANs that have assigned two VXLAN VNIs with their MAC addresses learned and advertised in EVPN EVI 1, and assigned a RD of 1, that then provides its unique ID across the fabric.

Okay, but one of the elements that you have to consider is EVPN routing in BGP. It relates to the various types of reachability information that EVPN will advertise into BGP. In the wonderfully named IETF document: *BGP MPLS Based Ethernet VPN* (https://tools.ietf.org/html/draft-ietf-l2vpn-evpn-11), this information is classed as *Network Layer Reachability Information* (NLRI).

BGP Route Types for EVPN

The need for NLRIs are to allow two BGP speakers in the fabric, which in this case are switches, to advertise their capabilities and make sure they're compatible so they can both communicate with and transport traffic between each other.

At the time of publication of this book, there are five route types supported for EVPN by Juniper Networks:

1. Ethernet Auto-Discovery (AD) Route: used for multi-path and mass withdraw.

2. MAC/IP Advertisement Route: used for MAC advertisements.

3. Inclusive Multicast Ethernet Tag Route: used for *BUM flooding (Broadcast, Unicast, and Multicast)*.

4. Ethernet Segment Route: used for ES (Ethernet Segment Discovery) and DF (Distributed Forwarder) Election.

5. IP Prefix Route: used for IP route advertisement.

Let's run through each route type in a little more detail in order to understand how EVPN interacts with BGP and provides transport over the fabric.

EVPN Type 1 Route: Ethernet Auto-Discovery (AD) Route

Auto-discovery is the process by which a leaf switch with a new route advertises the new route to the fabric and to all the other leaf switches that are part of the same EVPN segment. The advertised route has an ESI value, as well as an extended community value, so other leaves know which EVPN segment it belonged to. The community contains a flag that lets other switches in the fabric know if the traffic can be load-shared over multiple links or if it's a single link. If the flag is set to 1, that means only one link associated with the Ethernet segment can be used for forwarding. If the flag is set to 0, that means that all links associated with the Ethernet segment can be used for forwarding data. Basically it's the difference between active/active links or single active.

So if a remote leaf, (say Leaf 4, in Figure 9.7) receives an Ethernet auto-discovery route from Leaf 1 and Leaf 2 (as the server is dual-attached), it will look at the advertisement, see that it's for the RED EVPN segment (which it is a part of) and install that route into its table. It also knows it will have two VXLAN tunnels to forward traffic back over to Server 1, as both leaves and the VXLAN tunnels are in the same EVI (RED).

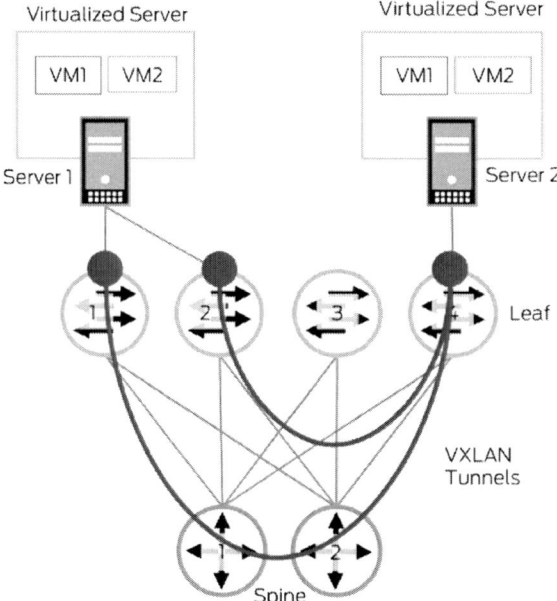

Figure 9.7   EVPN Type 1 Route

One benefit of the auto-discovery process is that in the event of a link failure convergence times can be a lot faster. Usually, when a link fails to a server, a leaf switch would withdraw each of its individual MAC Advertisements from that server. If that switch is holding thousands of MAC addresses for that link, the normal withdrawal process would mean issuing thousands of withdrawal notifications for all of those MAC addresses.

Because an auto-discovery route is associated with an interface as opposed to a single MAC address, a single withdraw route statement, say from Leaf 1 to Leaf 4, would tell Leaf 4 to remove all of the those MAC addresses it learned from Leaf 1. This means your convergence times are significantly reduced.

EVPN Type 2 Route: MAC/IP Advertisement Route

The purpose of a Type 2 route is to advertise MAC addresses it but it can also advertise IP addresses that are bound to the same MAC address. Take a look at Figure 9.8.

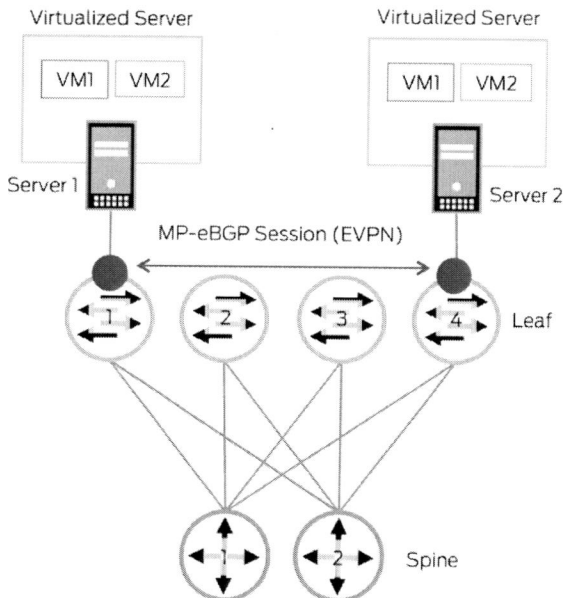

Figure 9.8   EVPN Type 2 Route

Using Figure 9.8, let's say that Leaf 4 learns the MAC addresses in the data plane from Ethernet frames received from Server 2. Once Leaf 4 learns Server 2's MAC address, it automatically advertises the address to other leaves in the fabric and attaches a route target community, which is the solid red circle in Figure 9.8.

Upon receiving the route, Leaf 1 has to make a decision as to whether it should keep the route. It makes its decision based on whether an import policy has been configured to accept red route targets. No policy, then the advertisement would be discarded.

So, at a minimum, each EVI on any participating switches for a given EVPN must be configured with an export policy that attaches a unique target community to the MAC advertisements, and also, it must be configured with an import policy that matches and accepts advertisements based on that unique target community.

EVPN Type 3 Route: Inclusive Multicast Ethernet Tag Route

To understand EVPN Type 3 routing in EVPN, you need to understand BUM traffic. BUM traffic is really broadcast traffic that in a normal network would be flooded to every node in the same VLAN/broadcast domain. In a Juniper Networks solution using EVPN/VXLAN, the switches in the fabric support ingress replication of BUM traffic, which means when BUM traffic arrives on a switch, that switch unicasts copies of the received BUM packets to each switch that belongs to the same EVPN instance, as opposed to just broadcasting the traffic everywhere.

Type 3 routes inform the remote switches in the fabric how BUM traffic should be handled. This information is carried in an attribute or feature within the VXLAN tunnel called *Provider Multicast Service Interface* (PMSI). This attribute specifies whether PIM (Protocol Independent Multicast) or ingress replication should be used to send BUM traffic.

This EVPN route is very simple. The route informs remote PEs of how BUM traffic should be handled and the information is carried in the PMSI Tunnel attribute. It specifies whether PIM or ingress replication will be used and the addressing that should be used to send the BUM traffic. So Leaf 2 advertises that it is expecting and using ingress replication and that Leaf 1 should use 4.4.4.4 as the destination address of the VXLAN packets that are carrying BUM traffic.

EVPN Type 4 Route: Ethernet Segment Route

Type 4 Routing solves two complications with overlay networking–first it helps in the designated forwarder election process and second, it helps add a new split horizon rule.

Okay, but what is designated forwarding and what is split horizon? Split horizon is the method of preventing routing loops by routing protocols from advertising a route back onto the interface from which it was learned.

Standard EVPN already has some default split horizon rules in place. For example, if a switch receives a BUM packet from a local server:

- It floods to servers in the same VLAN
- Floods to remote switches in the same VLAN
- But it will not flood to the original server that sent the BUM packet

If a switch in the fabric receives a BUM packet from another switch in the fabric:

- It floods to local servers in the same VLAN
- But won't flood to other switches in the fabric

The problem is that active/active connections across our fabric can break these rules. Earlier, in Type 1 Routing Ethernet Auto-Discovery, you learned that Type 1 can enable multipath forwarding when a server is dual-connected to two switches and when you are sending traffic over multiple links in a fabric. But while this is fine for unicast traffic, it's a little more problematic with BUM traffic.

For example, if Leaf 1 in Figure 9.8 makes a copy of the received BUM traffic from Server 1 and then sends a unicast copy of this packet to all leaf switches in the same EVPN instance, there is a likelihood that Server 2 will receive multiple copies of the same packet. The other potential issue is that you could start creating loops as traffic is forwarded back to the source. Again, using Leaf 1 as an example, it receives a BUM packet and sends a unicast copy to all switches in the same EVPN instance. Leaf 2 receives this packet and because of the split horizon rule forwards it back to the server that sent the original packet, thus creating a loop.

To resolve this problem, all of the switches in the same Ethernet segment, or EVPN, elect a designated forwarder for that Ethernet segment/EVPN. This is where Type 4 comes in as it helps with the DF election process and adds a new split horizon rule.

The election process consists of a series of switches in the same Ethernet segment (ES) creating a list of the all of the IP addresses of all the switches in the same ES. Each switch is given a value starting from 0, which is for the switch with the lowest IP address. Once a DF is selected, this switch or DF can forward BUM traffic. Other switches in the same ES that are not elected as the DF will drop BUM traffic.

EVPN Type 5 Routes

Type 5 routes for EVPN are generally seen in data center interconnect (DCI) scenarios. For example, let's say you have BMS Server 1 in one data center that needs to send traffic to BMS Server 2 in another data center. Now, our VXLAN tunnel needs to traverse the MPLS WAN network to keep the Layer2 domain between the two server applications.

So Leaf 1 receives the traffic from Server 1. The leaf encapsulates the Ethernet frames in to VXLAN and sends those packets to the edge router or gateway from this data center to the WAN. The edge gateway (let's say DC1 MX) will have an IRB interface that will act as the gateway address for Leaf 1.

The MX will strip off the VXLAN header and do a lookup on the remaining Ethernet packet, which will have a destination for Server 2 in DC2. The edge gateway strips the Ethernet header and routes the remaining IP packet based on the IP route table related to its IRB interface. The MX then uses a Type 5 route that it receives from its opposite number in DC2, and then forwards it over the VXLAN tunnel between DC1 MX and DC2 MX.

DC2 MX receives the VXLAN encapsulated packet, strips the VXLAN encapsulation off, routes the IP packet to its IRB interface and re-encapsulates the packet with a Ethernet header with a destination MAC address of Server 2. It does the MAC address lookup and forwards the packet over the VXLAN tunnel to the corresponding leaf and then to Server 2.

So in this scenario, Type 5 allows for inter-data center traffic to be forwarded over VXLAN tunnels, but allows the Ethernet MAC to be translated into IP.

Hopefully, these five types of EVPN routing explain how the EVPN signals in to BGP. The next element to understand is how the gateway is distributed across several switches.

MORE? Check out the Juniper TechLibrary for more about EVPN and Juniper switches such as these overviews: https://www.juniper.net/techpubs/en_US/junos/topics/concept/evpns-overview-ex9200.html; and, https://www.juniper.net/techpubs/en_US/junos15.1/topics/concept/evpns-overview.html.

Distributed Layer 3 Gateway

EVPN based fabrics have the ability to distribute Layer 3 gateways over several switches in the same way a normal Layer 3 gateway would be done, but for the overlay.

Using the example shown in Figure 9.9, you can see the IP Fabric with the leaf switches providing Layer 2 VXLAN gateway functions and the spine layer providing Layer 3 VXLAN gateway functions.

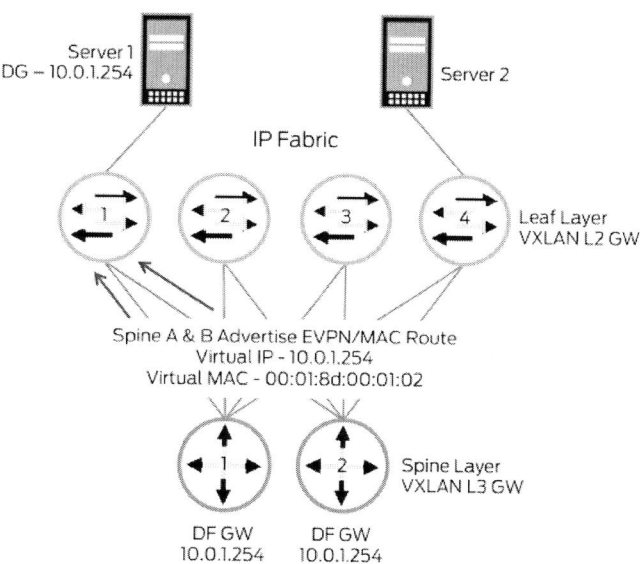

Figure 9.9   EVPN Distributing Gateways

Server 1 is configured with a default gateway address of 10.0.1.254. Both Spine A and B have been configured with the same virtual IP address of 10.0.1.254 and they share the same virtual MAC address of, say, 00:01:8d:00:01:02. Both Spine A and B will advertise both Type 1 Ethernet Segment IDs (ESI) as well as the Type 2 MAC addresses. The leaf layer switch will see equal-cost reachability to the same MAC and ESI, and as such, will load balance traffic over both links to both spines.

DC1 and DC2 EVPN Solutions

Okay, how does all this EVPN stuff apply back to the two design scenarios for DC1 and DC2?

Well, because EVPN is a protocol-based solution, its support is defined on the switches in our fabric, as is the VXLAN encapsulation. Meaning that for both solutions, the server layer would connect to the leaf devices (top-of-rack switches or end-of-row chassis) with VLAN connectivity. Those VLANs would be mapped to the relevant VXLAN VTEP on the switch ports and then that VTEP is mapped to the relevant EVPN instance providing that VTEP's Layer 2 domain. As mentioned before, you can map multiple VTEPs to either a single EVPN instance, creating a *one-to-one mapping*, or you can map multiple VTEPs to a single EVPN instance, creating a *many-to-one mapping*.

This provides you with the flexibility to map related applications and their associated VLANs together under a single EVPN instance to provide them with isolated Layer 2 connectivity. You can then replicate it for other application groups and in time allow for the introduction of tenanted-based solutions.

One aspect not touched upon is the management of this EVPN-VXLAN solution. Because it's protocol-based the configuration of these elements need to be managed. This can be done very easily through the use of Juniper's *Junos Space Network Director* platform, which provides IP fabric deployment and EVPN-VXLAN configuration and management.

NOTE   Junos Space Network Director is beyond the scope of this book, but look for its inclusion in a future *Day One: Data Center Management Fundamentals*.

The other benefit of EVPN not covered is the extension of Layer 2 between data centers, referred to as *data center interconnect* (DCI). While not covered in this book, it has been extensively covered in *Day One: Using Ethernet VPNs for Data Center Interconnect*, so please refer to this excellent *Day One* book at http://www.juniper.net/us/en/training/jnbooks/day-one/proof-concept-labs/using-ethernet-vpns/.

MORE?   For a really excellent overview of EVPN, refer to Chapter 6 in *The QFX10000 Series*, by Doug Hanks, and published in 2016 by O'Reilly Media. See: http://www.juniper.net/us/en/training/jnbooks/oreilly-juniper-library/qfx10000-series/.

NEXT   What to read next? Try visiting Juniper's *Network Design and Architecture Center for Data Center Networks* for an incredible amount of links, books, guides, and movies: http://www.juniper.net/documentation/en_US/design-and-architecture/index.html.

Summary

This has been a book about data center fundamentals and how Juniper Networks technology can build data centers. It glosses over very complicated topics and issues to give you a fundamental understanding so you can get started on day one.

Everything in this book is subject to change. *Please* make every effort to visit the Juniper links provided throughout these pages for the most up-to-date data sheets and specifications, as those details will change much faster than this book's ability to track them.

Juniper Networks is the home of many data center and data center interconnect solutions. This book attempts to favor none while trying to explain them all. Keep in mind that data center networking is still a complicated engineering science and no one quite agrees on the perfect data center – even the technical reviewers who helped proof this book had conflicting advice.

While the book has shown you the basics of how to build a data center, it stops very abruptly at an architected example, and it says nothing about data center *administration*, where CoS, analytics, automation, and orchestration rule. The author hopes to write that next book for this *Day One* series as soon as possible. Until that time, please use the Juniper website to track the many data center administration tools, from Juniper Contrail, to the NorthStar Controller, to Juniper cloud-based security products and analytics.